THE FLYING BANDIT

The FLYING BANDIT

HEATHER ROBERTSON

James Lorimer & Company, Publishers

Toronto 1981

Design: Artplus Ltd/Brant Cowie
Cover photo: Archives, University of Manitoba
Author photo: Arnaud Maggs

CANADIAN CATALOGUING IN PUBLICATION DATA
Robertson, Heather, 1942-
  The flying bandit

ISBN 0-88862-520-0   2. Robbers and outlaws.

1. Leishman, Ken, 1931-1979   2. Thieves - Canada -
Biography.   3. Bank robberies - Canada.   I. Title.

HV6248.L44R62   364.1'552'0924   C81-094738-2

James Lorimer & Company, Publishers
Egerton Ryerson Memorial Building
35 Britain Street
Toronto M5A 1R7, Ontario

Printed and bound in Canada

6   5   4   3   2   1   81   82   83   84   85   86

Contents

Preface

I'VE WANTED TO WRITE the story of the
Flying Bandit for more than ten years. About 1970, when Ken
Leishman was in prison serving eight years for his gold robbery and two jailbreaks, he asked me to edit his autobiography. We talked too about doing a radio drama and a movie.
Ken had written the rough draft of his life story in jail awaiting trial. It was unfinished. Authorities discouraged more
publicity; friends feared it would hurt Ken's chances for parole. Ken's manuscript was unpublished when his plane went
down in December, 1979, and he is now presumed dead.

Ken wanted his story told. He talked freely, without embarrassment, to police, reporters and friends. I have drawn
on these rich sources, and my own vivid memories, to piece
together the amazing story of Ken's escapades. In a few in-
stances where information is sketchy or contradictory, I have
surmised events based on the evidence available; I have also
created conversations to make the story more realistic and to
recapture its drama. *The Flying Bandit* is an adventure story
about real people and real crimes—incredible as they may
seem.

Heather Robertson

Acknowledgements

AMONG THE MANY PEOPLE who kindly assisted me with information and anecdotes about Ken Leishman, I am particularly grateful to Ken's mother, Irene Agarand, for her cooperation and encouragement.

The staff of the former *Winnipeg Tribune* generously allowed me access to the clipping file. Writer Sarah Yates-Howorth helped me with the research. An article by Stanley Handman in *Weekend Magazine,* vol. 8, no. 29, 1958, was a valuable source.

I am especially indebted to Mel Myers, Q.C., Judge Manly S. Rusen, Q.C. and to Roland Penner, Q.C., who read the manuscript and made available to me the transcript of the preliminary hearing on the gold theft charges. My thanks also to Grant Sinclair and Judge Pamela Sigurdson for their wise counsel.

My particular thanks to Cpl. Allan James Richards of the RCMP whose skills as an interviewer provided unexpected detail and excitement.

Prologue

WHERE IS THE FLYING BANDIT? Is he dead—or alive?

Did Ken Leishman—Canada's Scarlet Pimpernel—die in the crash of a light aircraft in 1979? Or did he disappear? Is he in hiding somewhere, living off the last of the twelve gold bars he stole from under the noses of the police?

The Flying Bandit—Canada's most popular thief—has disappeared into thin air.

It's not the first time.

Ken Leishman flew from Winnipeg to Toronto, robbed a bank and flew home with $10,000.

He spirited $400,000 worth of pure gold bullion away from the Winnipeg airport. It was the largest theft in Canadian history.

He escaped from jail, stole a plane and disappeared across the border. It was the largest jailbreak in Canadian history.

Ken was locked in an escape-proof cell. He escaped.

Ken always got caught. That was part of the game. His crimes were brilliant moves in a chess match with the police; if he didn't get caught, who would know about it? Ken Leishman became a celebrity, a folk hero, a modern Robin Hood. He stole from the rich to give to the poor, and *he* was the poorest guy he knew. He carried a gun but he never used it;

his capers were daring, flamboyant and fun. Ken lived his life as if it were a movie.

He was a gentleman thief, handsome, well-dressed, soft-spoken. He didn't smoke, swear or chase women. He was always polite. Ken could charm the birds out of the trees. He had style. He had class. Everybody who knew Ken loved him. Even the cops. Ken could talk his way into, and out of, almost anything, but beneath his confident, charismatic manner there was a childlike vulnerability, a perpetual innocence. People wanted to help him, take care of him, do things for him.

Ken was a romantic figure, a rebel, an outsider, a victim, the perfect symbol of an aggressive, ambitious, avaricious generation. Ken wanted to make it. Fast. He did. Had he gone straight, Ken could have been a corporation president or prime minister. By going crooked he became a legend.

This is the story of how he did it.

Holdup—
March 17, 1958

KEN LEISHMAN WIPES the traces of shaving cream from the corners of his moustache. It isn't much of a moustache, just a thin black line like a pencil mark breaking the pallor of his broad Belgian face, but he's had it ever since he could shave, fourteen, fifteen, even though the guys laughed at him. It makes him look older, sophisticated, gives him confidence.

"You look like Clark Gable," Elva had said on their first date. Wow! That was about the nicest thing anyone had ever said to him. Ken had seen every movie the King had ever made, two three times. Even as a little snotty-nosed kid in Treherne, Manitoba, he'd scrounge a nickel from his mom on Saturdays and sit in the dusty old movie theatre until the manager finally kicked him out, and later, when he was delivering groceries for Curry's store or cutting meat at Tommy Reece's butcher shop, he'd hitch the ninety miles into Winnipeg and blow a week's wages on a show, stuffing himself with popcorn and Cokes and hotdogs till he thought he'd throw up, but never filling those two hollow legs his mom said he had. Ken imitated Gable's swagger and his wide, lopsided grin. He combed his dark curly hair so one lock fell across his forehead, and he started wearing a soft, floppy snapbrim fedora tilted over one eye. He learned how to stare

3

at women sideways, lids drooping over laughing liquid brown eyes, bedroom eyes Elva had said, giggling and blushing red as her hair. After his hair had fallen out three years ago, when Ken was only twenty-three, he called his moustache the salt on the egg.

It's his trademark now, the thing everyone knows him by, the big bald guy with the moustache. Should he shave it off? He'd look younger without it, a totally different man. The perfect disguise. Ken hefts the razor. His hand trembles slightly. No, Elva would be upset, ask questions. It would call attention. Better to appear perfectly normal, pretend that nothing is unusual, be himself. It had worked last time.

Ken dresses carefully, crisp white shirt, grey flannel suit, dark tie, thick and soft to the touch, better than anything he's worn before. He'd picked the clothes out yesterday at Hanford-Drewitt, Winnipeg's ritzy men's shop, lucky to hit the end of winter sale. He'd tried on a honey of a navy blue three-piece chalk stripe, half-price, a real banker's suit, but there was no way Ken Leishman could pass for a banker, not with his six-foot one-inch frame on those broad shoulders, thick and muscled from pitching hay, his gnarled hands hanging out of the sleeves like two huge hams. No, he needed something conservative, inconspicuous, not the cheap salesman's suits he usually wore, clothes that made people feel a little superior to you, but a suit that inspired confidence, something sober, respectable, the kind of suit a wealthy contractor might wear to a meeting with his bank manager. He'd paid cash for the clothes and when he got home he cut all the labels out.

He opens his briefcase and tucks in a clean shirt. He pauses, his hand on the knob of the bureau drawer, head cocked, listening. Elva and the kids are in the kitchen. He can hear the chatter of little voices and smell the toast burning. Ken reaches swiftly into the drawer under the socks and shorts and slips out a small .22 automatic pistol. He holds it gently in a handkerchief and checks the chamber. Loaded. He wraps it in the handkerchief and slips it into the briefcase. A couple of file folders go in on top and he snaps it shut. Lots of room. If he needs the space, he can always throw the shirt out on the way home.

Elva is frying bacon and eggs. Ken feels a little sick. His stomach's in a knot. Wade, the baby, is screaming and Lee

Ann and Ron are yelling over the blare of the radio. An Irish jig. Golly, it's St. Patrick's Day! Ken crosses his fingers. My lucky day. Instinctively he closes his eyes and prays for the saint's blessing, then catches himself with a grin. It's been a dog's age since he darkened the door of an RC church, or any church for that matter, not since he was a kid and his grandma had a big row with the priest and turned Anglican. Not that the church ever did sweet f-all for Kenny Leishman, that's for sure. God helps those who help themselves.

"See you tonight," he says, giving Elva a hug and kiss. "Wish me luck."

A raw spring wind is blowing across the tarmac as Ken parks his black Cadillac in the members' lot of the Winnipeg Flying Club. He glances over to where his three-seater Stinson is parked. He'd thought about flying it to Toronto. Take too long. Besides he'll need all his energy. Let TCA do the work. They get paid enough for it. Ken feels a bitter surge of envy when he sees the sleek silver Super Constellation nosed up to the Winnipeg airport. He could fly that. Easy as pie.

All his life he'd dreamed of being a pilot, well, since the war anyway, when he'd stayed on his grandparents' farm south of Treherne. On hot summer days he'd lie on the Clydes' broad backs out in the pasture and watch the little yellow training planes wheeling in the blue sky over southern Manitoba and he'd dream he was up there shooting down Germans, bang! bang! He'd come home a hero, tall and proud in his sky blue air force uniform, the Victoria Cross on his chest, and he'd be welcomed back to Treherne by a marching band and all the kids who beat him up and called him names would stand in respectful silence while the people cheered and clapped and the girls crowded around giving him the eye. He'd be famous and he'd forgive them all for being so mean to him, even the Children's Aid worker who conned him into coming into Winnipeg to a foster home by promising to take him to the airport to see the planes and then when they got to the city said it was too late, the airport was too far away, he'd see them up in the sky anyway. Well, what had he expected? All he got from his life was a kick in the teeth. So what if TCA turned down his application for pilot training? He can fly rings around those birds. He's got his own airplane. He's got plans. All he needs is money.

"Another business trip, Mr. Leishman?" smiles the stewardess, handing Ken a candy on a silver tray.

"Yep," Ken winks. "Gonna make a killing this time."

He stretches out, knees pressed uncomfortably against the
seat in front, and closes his eyes. If only he could sleep, rest,
think clearly, keep his brain from spinning around like a fiery
pinwheel exploding in a shower of sparks. His hands are cold
and a small pulse of pain throbs at the base of his skull. God
he's tired. How long since he's really slept? Six, eight weeks?
In his excitement he'd lost all track of time, pacing the floor
half the night like a caged wolf, scribbling, scheming, planning, jumping out of bed to draw up blueprints, make lists,
flying two hundred miles north from Winnipeg to Moar Lake
four, five times a week, the Stinson groaning under the
weight of supplies for his fishing lodge, Leishman's Fly-In-
Lodge, the best in Canada—heck the best in North America
when it's finished . . . if . . . Maybe he'd been wrong to build
the lodge in the dead of winter, landing the plane on the lake
in the dark at thirty, forty below, the Indians lighting bonfires
of spruce branches to mark the spot, propping the skis on
logs to keep them from freezing into the ice, bedding down
on a pile of boughs in a tent half-buried in snow and waking
the next morning with his bald head like a block of ice,
thawing the plane with a blowtorch under the fuselage and
taking off again. He figured he'd been smart hiring local Indians to cut the logs. Good workers. Cheap. Jeez, those Indians went through a lot of groceries! He only hired a dozen
fellows but he'd had to feed their wives and kids too, while
the men were in the bush, and then they traded jobs around
so pretty soon he was feeding the whole damn reserve! He
hardly knew where the money had gone, $5,000 of his own
first, every cent he had in the world, then a big loan from a
finance company, then he'd started buying on credit. He figured he owed $20,000, maybe $25,000, he'd lost track. The
heavy stuff, the lumber, the generator, the stoves and septic
tanks, had to go in by tractor train over the winter road before
breakup. That gave him less than a month, at most, if he was
going to be operating by June . . . . he *had* to be. . . .

"Is it much farther?"

A woman's voice in his ear. High. Scared. Ken opens his
eyes. In the next seat an elderly woman in her Sunday best

is sitting bolt upright, staring straight ahead, clutching the arms of her seat in liver-spotted hands.

"Not much," Ken smiles. "First flight?"

He knows the answer even before she nods. Why are people so afraid? They miss so much! She should be dancing with joy!

"Look." He points out the window to the snow-covered lakes spread out beneath them like lace. "It's beautiful!"

She swallows and closes her eyes.

How many women like this has he known? A hundred? A thousand? Decent, respectable women, industrious, frugal, uncertain, anticipating the blows life might deliver before they fall, so isolated, circumscribed, they're grateful for the slightest attention, the smallest token of affection, even from a stranger. How many stainless steel cookware sets has Ken sold to these women, proffering a spatula or a strainer like a flower, fixing them tenderly with his brown eyes, dazzling them with his shiny pots and pans, playing on their responsibility, their economy, only $40 down and the rest on delivery, watching their eyes, gauging the hesitation, the doubt, the greed, the excitement that would tell him long before he finished his spiel that they were already thinking how necessary, how absolutely essential a set of Queen Anne ware was to a happy home, how delicious it would be to show it off, not realizing, or preferring to forget, that they were paying three times more than they would from the Eaton's catalogue but if they bought from the catalogue they'd settle for aluminum whereas this was a once-in-a-lifetime opportunity. A year ago Ken had been the best cookware salesman in western Canada.

His spirits rise as he talks to the woman, easing her panic and his own. He draws little pictures of his lodge on a napkin, the lounge in front, big windows facing the lake, a granite fireplace he's going to build himself, modern kitchen all stainless steel, flush toilet in each cabin, wall-to-wall broadloom. Nothing but the best. First class. The only five star rating in Manitoba. He'll advertise in the States, sporting magazines, rich Americans really go for this kind of thing, he'll fly them in himself, Elva'll cook, the kids will clean up, haul wood, Dad will keep the outboards running, he's a whiz at mechanical things, Indian guides, maybe family things later, scenic tours down the river, waterskiing. His pen speeds over the paper.

"My, it's grand." the woman says. "It must be very expensive."

Ken laughs out loud. "You can say that again!"

"You must be a wealthy man."

"Not yet."

Ken picks up a U-drive at the Toronto airport and drives up to Lund's sports store on Bayview. He orders ten fourteen-foot aluminum boats and ten eighteen-horse Johnson outboards. Eight grand. He writes a cheque for $3,000 down payment dating it the following day, March 18, 1958. The salesman doesn't seem to notice.

He's headed downtown by 1 p.m. cruising slowly through the lunch hour traffic. He stops on Yonge St., just north of Bloor St., in front of a small old-fashioned branch of the Bank of Commerce. He gets out, goes in quickly and speaks to the accountant at the desk. He would like to make an appointment with the manager. That afternoon, two o'clock. Business proposition. Name's McGill. Lawyer. Welland, Ontario.

Ken drives around the block and parks on Church Street facing south. He takes a half-empty bottle of rye out of his briefcase. Two quick slugs. The booze hits his empty stomach like red-hot iron. Come on, Kenny! This is it! You've got to do it! You gotta get that money now or you're gonna lose everything, the works, lodge, car, house, everything down the pipe, flat broke, back on the street flogging pots and pans, a two-bit hustler. This is it. Last chance. Once more. That's it. Set for life. What are you worried about? Lost your nerve? You pulled it off last time, a piece of cake, jeez, if only you'd asked for more dough, you dumb . . . !

Ken's first bank robbery was a sweetheart, a masterpiece, if he did say so himself, although he'd never told a soul, not even Elva. It had been exactly three months ago to the day, December 17, 1957, although it seemed when he thought about it, and he thought about it all the time, half a lifetime ago. He'd been desperate, almost as desperate as he is now.

The cookware company had folded on him, not a word of warning. He was out of work and in debt. He sold executive aircraft for a while, fancy four-seaters that paid a good commission, but nobody in Winnipeg was buying planes in December. He still owed on his Stinson, on his Caddy, on his house in River Heights, not in the ritzy part but on the fringe, near the railway tracks, facing an open field where he could land his plane after a trip out west taxiing right up to the front door. Didn't that knock the neighbours' eyes out! Ha, ha!

Everybody thought he was rich, winning all those prizes for sales, but there he was, a week before Christmas without a pot to piss in and Elva and the kids expecting big presents. How could he face them and say "Sorry, no Christmas this year. Your dad's a bum." Just like his own dad. He'd had too many rotten, stinking Christmases as a kid crying himself to sleep behind the kitchen stove because all he got was a pair of socks or some beat-up old toys from the Red Cross. His kids weren't going to suffer the way he had, he'd sworn to that. He made the rounds of the banks. No dice. Even the sleazy finance companies turned him down. He wouldn't mind so much if they'd come straight out with it. It was the excuses he hated, "We'll let you know tomorrow, Mr. Leishman." "Our credit manager has to look this over. I'm sure there's no problem." But there always was a problem. Well, he'd show them. If they wouldn't give him the money, he'd take it. Simple.

Ken's panic had suddenly evaporated. His mind worked clearly, coolly. He borrowed $200 from a buddy at the flying club and bought a return ticket on TCA to Toronto. He drove across the border to Fargo, North Dakota, bought his .22 automatic and smuggled it back taped to the inside of his leg.

He flew to Toronto December 16, 1957, booked into the Park Plaza and spent the afternoon drifting with the Christmas crowds up and down Yonge St. getting the feel of the place, judging the best time of day, when the crowds would be thick enough to conceal his escape but not so thick he couldn't move, watching where the cops were stationed, looking for the right bank. This wasn't going to be a bang, bang cowboy job but a cool, businesslike operation. Ken had it all figured out. The gun was just a prop, a demonstrator model, something to focus the bank manager's attention, freeze his mind, like a stainless steel double boiler, so he'd obey Ken's instructions.

Ken needed a very specific type of bank. It had to be one in which the manager's office had a single door and solid walls. He found it in the Toronto-Dominion bank at the corner of Yonge and Albert, just north of Eaton's. It was an old stone building, doing a brisk business, obviously a lot of cash on hand. He went back to the Park Plaza, called the bank and asked to speak to the manager.

"Mr. Lunn is busy at the moment," said the secretary.

"Fine," said Ken. "I'll call later."

At 2:30 p.m. the next day he parked his U-drive on Richmond Street two blocks south of the bank. He walked in nonchalantly, briefcase in one hand, a package of Christmas wrapping under his arm.

"May I speak to Mr. Lunn, please?" he asked the accountant. The manager was busy. Ken waited, leaning against the counter, kibitzing about the crowds, the weather. He felt no fear, only excitement. Finally the manager nodded from his doorway.

"Hiya," said Ken, sticking out his hand. "Name's Gair. Buffalo. I've got an interesting proposal I'd like to talk over with ya."

"Come in, please," said Mr. Lunn, stepping back. "Let me take your coat and hat." Mr. Lunn hung Ken's heavy black winter coat on the hall tree and carefully placed his black homburg on top. Ken watched him. A small, grey man, old, looks like he has heart trouble. Real "milktoast". Hope he doesn't croak on me.

"Mind if I close the door?" asked Ken.

"Go ahead. Please do." Mr. Lunn glanced at his watch. 2:40 p.m. He was tired. He hoped this didn't take too long.

Ken closed the door gently but firmly. The office was suddenly very quiet. Ken sat down in a green leather chair facing the manager's desk. He snapped open his briefcase.

"I have something unusual here to show you."

Mr. Lunn bent over wearily and pulled his chair closer to the desk. When he looked up he was staring down the barrel of Ken's gun. Ken spoke softly, intensely, almost soothingly.

"Mr. Lunn, as you obviously realize, this is a holdup."

Mr. Lunn's eyes were round. His mouth opened once, twice and closed. He cleared his throat.

"Yes. I see."

Ken continued to speak softly and clearly, never taking his eyes from Lunn's face.

"You have a gun?"

"Yes."

"Where?"

"In my drawer."

"And an alarm?"

"Yes." Lunn motioned to the wall behind his chair.

"There will be no need to use either, Mr. Lunn," Ken went on. "I don't want to hurt you. I have a simple request to make of you. If you go along with me you will be released un-harmed. You may then call the police. It will be up to them to apprehend me. Do you understand?"

Lunn nodded.

"What do you want?"

"How much money do you have in your office here?" Ken jerked the gun in the direction of the manager's drawer.

"None." Lunn smiled wanly.

"You make loans."

"Of course. We pay through the teller."

Mr. Lunn was puzzled. Did this thief think a bank manager handed out money from his own pocket?

"You can cash cheques?" said Ken.

"Yes."

"Make out a cheque."

"I'll have to move to do that."

"Okay. Move carefully."

Mr. Lunn reached gingerly into his right hand drawer. He pulled out the first object his hand touched. A wad of counter cheques.

"Make one out."

"How much?"

Ken didn't expect that question. Jeez, was this guy going to hand him the whole bank? Or was it a trap, a way of enticing him into asking for too much and alerting the teller? Most bank robbers got away with peanuts, a couple of grand, not worth the trouble. What should he ask for? The clock chimed 2:45.

"How much cash does your teller have in his drawer?"

Lunn pondered. He usually had up to $100,000 in ready cash but it had been a heavy day for withdrawals. There might be $40,000, $50,000. Did this fellow know that? He seemed kind of dumb, about banks anyway. Could he chance a lie?

Ken tapped his foot restlessly. Hurry up. Hurry up. Don't lose control. Don't give him time to think.

"Okay, $10,000," he blurted.

"Fine." Lunn picked up his pen. He wrote out the cheque.

"Now sign it."

Lunn looked at Ken in amazement.

"I can't."

"Why not?"

"I don't have $10,000 in my personal account." He managed another pale smile.

"I'll sign it," said Ken. He grabbed the manager's pen and scrawled an illegible signature across the bottom. Lunn initialed it. He was careful to hold the pen in a different spot.

"Put it back," Ken snapped, gesturing with his gun. Lunn slipped the pen into his breast pocket.

"Okay," Ken grinned, leaning back. "We'll stay here for five minutes. We're discussing business, remember? Then we'll go to the teller's cage. We'll cash the cheque. Then you'll go along with me to the street. When we're far enough away, I'll let you go. How's your wife?"

Lunn jumped.

"Fine."

"What's her name?"

"Gwen."

"Yours?"

"Alan. Al."

"Any kids?"

"Two."

"Great. Wish I had kids myself. Specially at Christmas. Christmas is for kids, don't you think, Al? Are yours going to be home for Christmas?"

"We're going to Vancouver. See my daughter and our new grandson." Lunn reached instinctively towards his breast pocket where he carried colour photos of the baby. It was silly of him, showing them around. . . .

"Don't do that!" Ken sprang to his feet and held the gun against Lunn's left side, just under his rib. He handed Lunn his coat and hat, put on his own hat, picked up his package and briefcase and threw his coat over his arm, just covering the pistol. Lunn opened the door. Ken stayed by his side.

There were two customers in front of the single teller. Mr. Lunn stood in line, Ken pressed against his left arm.

"Golly, Al, that's great news about the baby!" Ken boomed. "You must be tickled pink. Or should I say blue, I guess, if it's a boy. Ha, ha!"

Lunn stared straight ahead at the teller. A young fellow, Les Steadman, new on the job. If only he'd look up! But Les was frantically counting out bills, toting up a passbook, aware that the manager's eyes were on him. Better not goof up. Five minutes to close and he was hopelessly behind. Catch it for sure. He barely glanced up as Mr. Lunn and his friend approached the wicket—at least Les assumed it was a friend because he kept calling Mr. Lunn "Al" and nobody in the bank ever called him anything but Mr. Lunn.

"Easy," Ken murmured, nudging the gun into Lunn's side.

Mr. Lunn pushed the cheque towards Les.

Les opened his cash drawer.

"How would you like it, sir?"

"Tens, twenties," said Ken. "Whatever's easiest."

Les looked into his drawer. It would just about clean him out.

"I'll have to go to the vault, sir. Won't be a minute."

Ken leaned against the counter swallowing hard. This was it. Game over. Cops would be there any second now. No, here was Les coming back, a wad of bills in his hand.

"Fifties okay?" he asked, slipping off the elastic bands.

"Fine," said Ken, opening his briefcase.

The saliva collected under his tongue as he watched Les count off two hundred bills. Les slipped an elastic around them and shoved them under the glass.

"Here you are, sir."

Jeez, is that all? Ken was astounded. It hardly made a dent in the wad! That wad was six, seven inches thick. A measley ten grand! Chicken feed! What a fool he'd been!

"Thank you," he grinned, putting the money in his brief-case with his left hand. What to do? Pull the gun and grab the rest? Must be another seventy, eighty grand in that roll. He stood stock still watching Les slip the elastics around the wad. All he had to do was reach out. . . .

The clock chimed three. The accountant was locking the front door. Oh, oh. Better get out of here.

"Come on, Al. Buy ya a coffee." Ken slipped his gun into his pocket and put his arm around Lunn steering him towards the door.

They came out into the damp cold. A miserable Sally Ann Santa was standing by a metal drum clanging a forlorn bell. Ken tucked a $10 bill into the drum. He took Lunn's elbow and steered him south towards Queen Street. Holy cow! A cop on the corner! Just his luck. Ken stepped quickly between Lunn and the cop, brushing the officer's back as they crossed Queen St. with the light. They turned the corner, Ken short-ening his stride, trying not to run, Lunn trotting to keep up, propelled by Ken's big hand clamped around his elbow. Ea-ton's loudspeaker was blaring "Silent Night."

"You're an educated man," said Lunn over the noise. "Why don't you get a decent job?"

Ken laughed.

"This is my job, Mr. Lunn."

They turned up a deserted lane and stopped.

"This is where I leave you," said Ken. "You will walk down the lane and not look back. Things have gone so well it would be a shame to kill you now."

Lunn nodded. He didn't want to die. Not in a dirty lonely lane among the garbage cans. He turned.

Ken held out his hand.

"Thanks, Al."

Lunn shook his hand. Ken watched him walk rapidly down the lane. He darted between two buildings and across a park-ing lot to where his car was waiting at a meter. He hopped in and drove south on Bay Street to Union Station. He put the gun in the briefcase, locked it and shipped it special delivery to his Winnipeg address.

He could hear police sirens as he walked back to his car. The hairs rose on the back of his neck. He was hot in his heavy coat, sweating. He felt like a sore thumb. The other men on the street were wearing light gaberdine top coats. Ken walked quickly across the street to the Royal York Hotel. In the men's wear store downstairs he bought a snazzy beige all-weather coat and a snappy brown stetson. In the washroom he wrapped his black coat, hat and silk scarf in two layers of Christmas paper and tucked the package under his arm.

A patrol car passed Ken's U-drive on the airport expressway. Ken slowed down, dropping back behind another car. The cops went on. Whew. So far, so good. He turned the car radio up loud and sang carols.

Ken got to the airport gate just as the 5 p.m. Winnipeg flight was loading. He half expected to see the place swarming with cops. Not one. His legs turned to water as he sank into his seat. Jeez, I've done it! I've done it!

"Christmas shopping?" smiled the stewardess, nodding at the package.

"Yeah," Ken grinned. "You might say that."

The briefcase arrived the next day. Ken paid the arrears on the mortgage, put a grand against the Caddy and two against the Stinson. He bought out Eaton's toy store for the kids. This was going to be a Christmas! He bought Elva a mink stole, pale brown to set off her hair, just like a real River Heights lady, and got a diamond signet ring for himself. Flashy, sure, but he was a salesman, wasn't he? The best goddamned salesman in the world!

Ken checked every page of the *Winnipeg Tribune*, half expecting to see his own face staring out at him. Not a line. Nothing in the *Free Press* either. Just as well. But he felt a little disappointed all the same. How many guys pulled a holdup like that? The next day he went into Dominion News, pretending to look at sports magazines, and picked up the *Toronto Telegram*. There it was, a front page banner headline: "Five Holdups in 24 Hours" Five! You mean there were four other guys robbing banks in Toronto yesterday? Ken couldn't believe it. Sure enough. Two guys cleaned an Etobicoke housewife out of $8,000, a thug gunned down a jeweller on Bay Street, a pimply kid got $2,000 up on Dupont, a "debonair" thief made off with $1,300 from the Royal Bank—ah, there, the lower right hand corner, a small story, a "dapper" bandit, no description, no details. Ken put the newspaper back. Golly, what if they'd all decided to rob the same bank at the same time! What a sideshow! He felt a little foolish. Robbing banks was getting crowded. Well, nobody else got $10,000. Better to keep it quiet, let it blow over.

Ken bought one last present, a cheap Christmas card with a big red laughing Santa on the front. He addressed the envelope to Mr. A.J. Lunn, Toronto-Dominion Bank, Yonge and Albert, Toronto, and inscribed inside:

"Merry Christmas. From a Satisfied Customer."

The bank robbery had really been the start of Ken's troubles, not the end. He'd flown the family down to Texas for a Christmas holiday, Elva with Wade and Blair in the front seat, Lee Ann, Ron and Dale in the back with the baggage. Sure, it was against safety rules but rules were for sucks. If he obeyed them all he'd never get off the ground, and besides it was a howl watching people's faces at the little whistle-stop airports when two big adults and five kids piled out of that plane like clowns out of a car at the circus. It made them a lot of friends.

It was while they were flying back from Texas that the idea for the lodge struck Ken like a bolt of lightning, the way most of his great ideas did. If he could fly 2,000 miles south for a holiday, why couldn't the Americans fly north? Texas was full of millionaires. When they found out Ken was a Canuck, all they talked about was fishing. Ken knew buzz all about fishing but ten years ago he'd spent a month working at Ken Whitie's lodge near Kenora before he bust his ankle, so he strung them along with stories about muskies so strong they pulled a canoe for miles and giant fighting bass that wore a guy out as much as a 700-pound tuna. The Yanks just lapped it up! They were nuts for fishing, he had a lot of good contacts, he could fly them all the way from Texas but most had their own planes. . . .

The idea took hold of him like an obsession. This was what he'd been looking for all his life, stability, security, independence, a real future. He got his hands on every map of northern Manitoba he could find and then he flew, cruising just over the treetops, criss-crossing the province day after day. When he found the right lake the government was only too happy to give him a ninety-nine year lease. He figured he could get the place built, the shell anyway, in time for the fishing season, he'd charge plenty, $75, $100 a day, make a bundle, pay off his debts by October, fix the place up the next winter, wouldn't cost more than $15,000, $20,000 to open. . . .

Ha! Twenty grand wouldn't get him a shack up there! Ken found that out too late. He went looking for partners. Sure, they said. Great idea! Can't miss! We'll give you the dough, you give us control. Shove it, said Ken.

So here he is back in Toronto. Jeez, if he'd only taken the big wad the first time he would have been laughing! Well, he'd learned his lesson. This time he's going for $40,000. Minimum. He takes another pull at the bottle of rye. The liquor makes him dizzy, lightheaded. It doesn't stop the dull throbbing in his skull. He never did have a head for booze.

One fifty p.m. Ken shoves the bottle back in his briefcase under the shirt. Okay, Kenny, let's get going. He walks the short block to Yonge and Bloor. He's soaked with sweat. Why did he wear his heavy black coat? Dumb. Too late now. He pauses irresolutely on the corner. An old con once told him the odds on the first job are seventy-thirty in the crook's favour. On the second job they're fifty-fifty. Fear sits like a stone in his gut.

He approaches the bank through a shoving swirl of pedestrians. Lunch hour crowds. Who would knock over a bank on the corner of Canada's busiest intersection at noon? Ken laughs. Ken Leishman, that's who!

Sharp at 2 p.m. Ken's asking for the manager, Howard Mason. He waits, calm, friendly, his warm bright eyes casually scanning the office. Varnished wood. Frosted glass. Good. Oh oh. The manager's office has a second door, at the back, opening into the staff area behind the cages. He hadn't seen that. He tenses, poised to run. Still time. Try somewhere else. Getting late though. Rouse suspicion. No problem. He'll close both doors.

"Hiya!" he grins at Mason, sticking out his hand. "McGill, contractor. Welland. Like to open an account here."

Howard Mason is a middle-aged tweedy man with a ruddy face, small moustache and a precise, tidy manner, a military manner Ken realizes later, when it's too late.

"What can I do for you, Mr. McGill?" Mason asks, closing the door.

Ken glances towards the other door. Jesus! There is no other door! It's been taken off its hinges. A young accountant is working at his desk not ten feet away.

"A safety precaution," Mason shrugs. "We've had a rash of robberies here lately."

Ken's hands are ice. His head is pounding. Get out of here! Get out of here! a voice at the back of his brain is screaming. Quick! Quick! I can't! I can't! another voice screams back. Last chance! Last chance!

"You can trust O'Brien," says Mason. "He's perfectly reliable."

Ken sinks into a chair. Time to think. Think. Think. Bluff it through.

He pushes his chair back until it is out of the accountant's line of vision. He opens his briefcase.

"I have some reports here I'd like to show you, Howard," he smiles, reaching in. "I think you'll find it a very unusual type of business."

Ken pulls out his gun and levels it at Mason's chest.

"Howard," he says quietly, "I'm sure you realize that this is a holdup. If you remain calm and pretend that everything is normal, no harm will come to you. We will do our business. Then you will leave the bank with me and I will release you. You have nothing to fear. Now I want you to show me the location of your alarm and gun."

Mason sits bolt upright, his hands on the desk, his face blank with surprise.

"This is ridiculous!" he cries suddenly, jumping up. "I won't stand for this!" he bolts towards the open door. Ken covers the distance between them in two strides. He grabs the front of Mason's jacket, feeling the button between his fingers and raises his gun.

"Hey!" cries Mason. The accountant glances up. Mason pulls back. The button comes off in Ken's hand. Mason darts through the open door.

"Police! Sound the alarm!"

Ken wheels and runs out the other office door. He charges through the bank, hardly seeing where he is going, out the front door, turns south on Yonge towards Bloor, running hard, dodging knots of secretaries, idling, chattering, blocking his way, shoppers drifting, peering, getting in his way, a mob of people waiting for the light to change. Green! There it goes. Ken runs faster, makes the light, dodging cars, dipping and weaving, horns blaring, somewhere behind him a hullabaloo, people shouting, he's running down Yonge now, panting hard, blood pounding in his ears, shoving people aside. There! A movie house. The Uptown. He'll hide here.

His right ankle catches something, buckles, gives. He loses his balance. Falling. Arms flailing. Gun drops. Got to find it. He hits the sidewalk hard, coat over his head, smothering, can't breathe. Got to get out. He fights to get free. Someone is holding his arms. A terrible weight on his back. He writhes and twists, throws off the weight, fights free of the coat, jumps up, and looks straight into the barrel of a revolver.

The cop shoves Ken against a parked car and cuffs his hands behind his back.

"I've got his gun! I kicked it away!" A grey little man in a clergyman's collar is holding Ken's gun with two fingers, by the barrel, as if it were a snake.

A young man in shirt sleeves, tie askew, chest heaving, is holding Ken's hat, crushed now and brown with grit. It's the man who tripped him, Ken O'Brien, the young accountant from the bank.

Elva Leishman is wondering whether to bake an apple or a raisin pie. There's lots of time, it's not five o'clock yet. Ken won't be home till eight or so. He always likes a big meal after a business trip, especially if things have gone well . . . .

"Mummy!" Lee Ann bangs in the front door, six-year-old Dale in tow. Her voice is urgent, angry.

"The kids said Daddy's a bank robber!"

"That's just silly!" Elva laughs, her heart sinking like a stone. "They made it up."

"Their mums heard it on the radio!" howls Dale. "They said it's true!"

"It's not true, is it mummy?"

"No," says Elva, puzzled. There had been trouble before, nasty gossip, but not here, in this neighbourhood, and never with the kids.

The phone rings. Elva can hardly hear through the buzzing in her head. The *Tribune*. Ken arrested. Daring daylight holdup. Does she have any comment?

"No!" Elva snaps, angry. "I don't understand what this is all about. Ken went to Toronto on business. Ken's not a . . . a . . . hoodlum. He wouldn't hurt a fly. He's just a wonderful guy!"

The phone rings again. John Harvard, the tough, abrasive reporter at CJOB. Is it true Ken was in financial trouble? Is it true he has a record? I don't know, Elva says. I never pry into Ken's affairs. He's a perfect husband and father. The *Free Press* calls. CKRC. CKY. Elva is crying now.

"I don't care what happens," she says. "I'll stand by Ken!"

She turns on the radio, half afraid. The deejay is shouting. Ken. Gun. Jail. She hears her own name, the children's names and ages, her comments on the phone, the fact that she's pregnant, a description of their Cadillac, the Stinson, even their address, 874 Lindsay St. How had they found all this out? Why doesn't Ken phone? Why don't the police phone? There must be some mistake. Ken wouldn't rob a bank. They had plenty of money!

The phone keeps ringing. Low, threatening voices. Shrill women's voices calling her awful, dirty names. What is happening?

Elva bundles the kids into their boots and snowsuits and shoos them out the front door. Lee Ann is back in two minutes.

"Mummy, there's a man taking our picture."

A small man with sparse red hair is bent on one knee on the front sidewalk furiously snapping pictures of the kids beside their snowman.

"Bring the kids in right now!" she says to Lee Ann. "Quick!"

Elva peeps out the picture window from behind the drapes. Half a dozen people are standing out in front staring at the house. Cars are creeping slowly past bumper to bumper. She watches them stop, people pointing, then drive on. When she sees the same blue Chevy come by for the third time she starts to feel sick. She draws the drapes and locks the doors.

Poor Elva. Poor Elva. Ken sobs, terrible uncontrollable tears of shock, misery, pain, the throbbing in his knee nothing compared with the pain in his heart, the sharp relentless agony of humiliation, not the humiliation of being caught, and caught so ignominiously, he could take that, but the humiliation of remorse. Elva was everything good and beautiful in his life. She loved him, believed in him, trusted him. And he had betrayed her. He would never be able to look her in the face again. A crook. A thief. A no-good bum. He huddles in a corner of his cell, head in his hands, wishing he could die.

Inspector William Bolton, head of the Toronto police department's Flying Holdup Squad, is humming to himself. It had been a good day, a lucky day for a change, a knock-out of a crime, the kind of stuff the public loves, nobody hurt, bugger falling right into their hands, plop, without having to lift a finger, dozens of witnesses, excitement, keep the press off their backs for a while. They could use some good press, the Toronto police. They'd looked like such assholes last Christmas, five robberies in one day! One guy killed. The Flying Squad had been formed right after that cucumber'd walked out of the Toronto-Dominion with ten grand. They still hadn't a clue.

When Bolton first saw Ken he though they'd nabbed some shark from Buffalo or Chicago up on a little family business— diamond ring, homburg, gun, Hollywood moustache. But who ever heard of a goon who said please and thank you? Or cried buckets in his cell? Or carried his wallet in his pocket, complete with driver's license, charge card and birth certificate? Or who packed a rod that had never been fired. And never fired it. Maybe he was what he said, a businessman driven nuts by money troubles, wife knocked up, debts. People do some funny things. Panic. Had to feel sorry for the guy. Only twenty-six. It's really not much of a case. Attempted robbery. Guy hadn't even asked for money. If he hadn't pulled the gun ... good lawyer'll get him off with a year or two, time off for good behaviour, out in no time.

Bolton puts in a routine call to the Winnipeg police. William Kenneth Leishman. Want him for anything? The officer sounds puzzled. Never heard of him.

"Run a check on him, will you?"

"Sure."

Bolton is surprised when Winnipeg calls back. William Kenneth Leishman: convicted on two counts of break, enter and theft in 1950. Sentenced to a year in the Manitoba provincial jail at Headingley. Nothing since.

Bolton orders up all the files on Toronto's unsolved robberies. There are a lot of them. He sighs as he leafs through them. Only two really fit Leishman's description: a Royal Bank holdup on December 16, 1957 and the Toronto-Dominion job December 17, 1957. Bolton reads carefully. White. Male. Tall. Well-built. Moustache. Dark coat, hat, white scarf. Late thirties, early forties. How do you start looking for a guy like that? Can't pull in half the executives in Toronto. The age is wrong but . . . Bolton begins to sniff a scent.

An hour later he's almost certain. Same style, same words, same clothes, although it's hard to believe a guy with that kind of imagination wouldn't change his appearance. He has a couple of fingerprints from Lunn's pen. Smudged. Risky. Good lawyer'd get them thrown out. Bolton has been around long enough not to take anything for granted. He's seen too many bastards get off because some smart ass cop *thought* he had a case. Get your man and *convict* him. That's what Bolton tells his squad. Case isn't closed till he's in the can. Christ, you got to be a goddamn lawyer in this business, all for a crummy $7,000 a year, outsmarting the best legal minds in the business pulling down fifty grand, living in Rosedale, defending *criminals* for Chrissakes. No sir, Bolton doesn't want to take chances with this one. Trials are messy. Lotta work. Time. Bolton wants a confession. Guilty plea. Safe, quick and easy. He pushes his buzzer.

"Johnson?"

"Yes, sir."

"Can you come to my office?"

"Yes sir."

Ken is surprised the cops treat him so well. Polite. Offer him cigarettes even though he doesn't smoke. Mattress on his cot. He feels funny sitting there quietly in his little cage watching the cops run around, typing up reports, answering the phone, yakking. All because of him! He's created quite a stir! Like putting his foot in an anthill and watching them scurry in all directions. It had been like that too when he was arrested, squad cars screaming up from all directions, cops running up, hundreds of them, waving their guns, traffic at a standstill, people jumping out of their cars, yelling, pushing, a huge mob gathering, people back in the traffic jam leaning on their horns. Jeez, what a row! Then a big procession as he was led back to the bank, cops shoving people out of the way, everyone gawking, shouting, Ken moving along in a little bubble of space like Moses parting the Red Sea for God's sake! He would have laughed if he hadn't felt himself slipping into a black pit, sobs gathering at the back of his throat. He'd always cried easily. Couldn't help it. He was afraid that if he started crying there on the corner of Yonge and Bloor he'd start to scream and never stop.

He's calm now. Relaxed. Everything's gone. Lodge. Money. Marriage. So. A great weight of worry has been lifted from his shoulders. Nothing more to lose. He can sleep now. Rest. He's so tired. Too tired to think. Care. Idly he watches the cops go about their business. Young guys. Good-looking. He'd wanted to be a cop once. Applied to the RCMP eight years ago, before he was married, before. . . . He never heard back. Funny about fate.

A young constable, hardly more than a cadet, brings Ken his dinner. Steak, potatoes, peas, corn, apple pie. Golly, it smells good! Ken wolfs it down. The constable—what's his name? Jack . . . ? Johnson? Johnson—sits at a desk in front of Ken's cell and brings out some paper work. The lights are on now. It's very quiet.

"You follow hockey?" says Johnson.

"Sure."

Heck, Ken never missed a game on TV. That was his Saturday night, a couple of beers, Elva making popcorn, Beliveau, Howe, the Rocket, Plante. Plante, he was the greatest. Ken always felt the goalie had the toughest job.

Johnson turns on a small radio, very low. They kibitz a bit about hockey, the Leafs, how they could never get a really great team with all that dough. It's been years since Ken's listened to the game on radio, since he was a kid. It's more exciting, your imagination sort of takes over. . . .

"You can make a phone call if you like," Johnson says at the end of the second period.

Ken shakes his head. Elva. What can he say? He feels the tears welling up again.

"You'll need a lawyer."

Ken shakes his head. Nothing he can do now. Get it over with. He feels like he's already disappeared. The world is spinning out of control.

"Coffee?"

"Sure. Thanks."

The coffee tastes like dishwater but it warms him up. Nice of the kid.

"Can't complain about the hospitality," Ken grins.

Johnson smiles.

"You're something of a celebrity around here. That job last Christmas was one slick operation, let me tell you. You really had us chasing our tails! Boy, did we look dumb! Ha! That took real guts."

Ken flushes. Praise from an expert! He shrugs.

"I was lucky that time."

Ken realizes he's been suckered only after he meets with his lawyer the next day. The lawyer is a real hot-shot, so his buddy in Winnipeg has said, convincing Ken that a good lawyer could mean the difference between two years and twenty. The lawyer's a homely guy, hornrimmed glasses, not too well dressed. What can you expect on legal aid? Perry Mason? Ken finds it hard to follow the jargon but the lawyer seems optimistic.

"I'll bring in a shrink," he says. "Psychiatry. That's the big thing now. Crummy childhood. Did you have a crummy childhood?"

"Yeah!" says Ken. "Sure did!"

"Good," says the lawyer. "Poverty. Neglect. Born in 1931. Terrific. Drought. Depression. Great stuff. Treatment. Rehabilitation. That's the thing now. Without that gun I'd probably get you off. Well, at least you didn't get any dough."

"What about the ten grand?"

The lawyer blinks. Ken patiently tells him the same story that he told Inspector Bolton that morning, how the December job had gone perfectly except he didn't take enough money.

"You see, if I'd taken $40,000 the first time, I wouldn't have had to come back. That was my big mistake."

The lawyer slowly removes his glasses and rubs his eyelids with the tips of his long fingers. His face is expressionless. Ken is disappointed. He'd expected some reaction. Appreciation. It *was* a smart job. . . .

The lawyer rubs his glasses with his handkerchief. In the long silence that follows it dawns like a tiny prick of light on the horizon of Ken's imagination that however obvious his guilt may have seemed to him it had not, perhaps, been quite as evident to the Toronto police and that in fact they may not have been able to prove any connection between the robberies at all.

"They'd have got me anyway," Ken says belligerently.

The lawyer replaces his glasses and closes his briefcase.

"That," he says, "is my business."

Ken is transferred to the stinking old Don Jail. He's stripped, showered, sprayed with louse powder and shoved into a cage with other prisoners awaiting trial.

"Hiya, Kenny!"

"How's the boy?"

"Welcome to the pit!"

Whistles. Catcalls. Cheers. Ken shrinks back, fists clenched, fearing ridicule, violence. The men press around offering cigarettes, chewing gum, chocolate bars, badgering him with questions, compliments, advice. Ken's confused, embarrassed. Gee, these guys like him! They're old pros, some of them in for the fourth, fifth time, records as long as your arm, yet they admire him! They've seen his picture in the papers. They knew more about him than he does! He's a hero!

On April 8, 1958 Ken Leishman pleads guilty to one charge of armed robbery and one charge of attempted armed robbery. On April 17 he is sentenced to three years for the attempted holdup of the Bank of Commerce, nine years for the Toronto-Dominion robbery in December. Consecutive. Twelve years. He is taken from the Toronto courtroom in handcuffs, shackled to a chain of convicts and driven to Kingston penitentiary. A month later he is transferred to Stony Mountain penitentiary outside Winnipeg. His spectacular career in crime is just beginning.

CHAPTER
TWO

Breakout

KEN IS SHOCKED when Elva brings her scrapbook of newspaper clippings on one of the visiting days. It's like reading about a stranger. All those pictures! His own face on the front page! He feels naked, embarrassed. "The Flying Bandit" the Winnipeg press has dubbed him, like he'd done something really spectacular. Heck, the robbery had been a botch, a mess! Why all this fuss? Ken feels like a fool. He's so used to getting the sharp end of the stick, he doesn't really expect anything else. In fact, like the prison doctor said, maybe he even looks for it, bringing trouble on his own head like the little guy in Li'l Abner with the cloud raining in his face all the time. Ken Blfspk, that's him. Loser.

His grandparents had told him his misfortunes were sin, but Ken didn't buy that, even as a little kid. He always had a practical mind. How could a six-year-old kid be responsible for his miseries? If it wasn't him then it was God, so to hell with God. Ken decided it was just luck.

His mom and dad had eloped in September, 1928, a year before the Crash, although things had looked rosy then. His mom, Irene, was a farm kid, only sixteen. His dad, Norman Leishman, eighteen, a good-looking guy in his cowboy duds, likeable, but shiftless. He went from one job to another around rural Manitoba, hired hand, salesman, caretaker, but he never seemed to settle into anything and when hard times came he was out of work. Ken was the second kid, born at the worst time, July 20, 1931, delivered on a bed of newspapers on his grandparents' farm south of Holland, Manitoba. He often said to his mom later, when things were going wrong, that she should've wrapped him up and thrown him in the garbage right then.

The only time his old man showed up was for a quick fuck. Ken sure never saw much of him. Or his money. Every cent his dad could hustle went for booze or tail. "Tiddles," they called him, "Tiddles" Leishman, after an old alley cat. That's what he was too. Oh, he had big ideas. Plans. Always looking for a job he never got, said his mom. They drifted around the country towns, Holland, Treherne, Rathwell, living in dirty rented rooms on relief. Fourteen bucks a month. Six for food, seven for rent, one for wood. His mom used to unravel the old woollen sweaters that came in the Red Cross parcels, wash the wool and knit them up again so they looked like new. Golly, she could knit beautiful stuff! She'd put the sweater on display in the local store and sell raffle tickets on it, twenty-five cents each. She'd make quite a lot of money, ten, twelve dollars sometimes. She worked hard to keep them going, cook, housekeeper, chambermaid, but sometimes when she boarded out there was no room for kids, not for Ken anyway. He was farmed out with friends, relatives, passed around from hand to hand like an old shoe, another unwelcome mouth to feed. One year he was in seven different homes. His mom would come to see him whenever she could but often weeks would go by and he'd think she'd died or forgotten him.

Ken couldn't remember much about his childhood except pain. Loneliness. Fear. You could see it in his eyes, even as a little kid, a faraway quizzical look like he was wondering why nobody wanted him. He was a good boy, bright, good-natured, polite. He didn't lie or steal or fight unless he was picked on. But he got whipped anyway. No matter how hard he tried things seemed to go wrong. He almost drowned. He broke his arm. He was kicked in the head by a horse. He scalded his chest taking the cap off a boiling tractor radiator. He was thrown from a runaway sleigh on an icy road and knocked unconscious. At least in the hospital they made a fuss over him. It was warm there and the food was good.

One spring when Ken was about eleven he'd been sent out in short pants and bare feet to herd the cows to the community pasture. It was freezing and the ice on the road turned his feet blue. His grandparents drove by, picked him up in their truck and took him to their farm. Not that they had any love for kids, especially not "Leishman's kids." Pauline and Albertine Agarand were Belgian, peasants, hard-headed, tight-fisted and proud. Ken was treated more like a hired hand than a grandson. He was up at dawn milking, shovelling shit from the barn, chopping wood, picking weeds, harnessing the horses, pitching hay, working on the threshing crew at harvest, picking eggs, cleaning chickens in the fall until the stench of singed feathers was burned into his skull forever. He didn't mind the work. He was a big, strong kid and glad to be useful. It never occurred to him to ask for money. When his grandparents sold the farm in 1945 and moved into Treherne they gave Ken a pair of skis. He couldn't ski. He'd never had time to learn.

Ken quit school at fourteen, halfway through grade seven. He didn't care. The teachers figured he wouldn't amount to much anyway. He had no real home now. His mom and dad had split up, his mom had remarried. His stepfather made it plain he didn't want Ken around. So Ken went to work for himself. The war was on, men were scarce, there were plenty of jobs for a willing boy. Tommy Reece took him on as a butcher's apprentice, cutting roasts, smoking, curing, making sausage. Ken was keen, energetic, quick with his hands. Reece said he could clean a turkey in the blink of an eye. Ken could have stuck at it, had a good trade, maybe even have bought Reece out, stayed in Treherne, become a pillar of the community, but he'd had enough dirty work. He hated the sight of blood spouting from the slashed throat of some squealing pig. He hated the stink of warm guts. Besides his dad had turned up. Flashy clothes. Big car. Norman Leishman was in the elevator business now, in Winnipeg. He needed an assistant. How about it?

Ken jumped at the chance. He had never been in an elevator, except the kind you put grain into, but heck, he'd tried his hand at so many things, fixing elevators should be a cinch. His dad talked about starting his own business, construction boom on, buildings getting taller, everybody needing elevators. The coming thing. Couldn't miss. They'd be millionaires. Ken went to Winnipeg to work for his dad.

He looked a lot older than sixteen. It was more than his fuzzy little moustache, or the grown-up clothes he wore, suits and ties and shiny shoes too big for his skinny frame. It was the way Ken carried himself, tall and straight, like he'd learned in air cadets, with a don't-touch-me look that created space around him, a charmed circle that drew people irresistibly into it. He was shy, awkward, handsome except for his nose which looked exactly like Bob Hope's. It made him look sometimes like a clown, especially when he laughed, but that didn't hurt. He'd learned long ago to hide his hurts in his eyes, to smile, smile, smile, even when his heart was breaking, to be cool, polite, deferential, to present a mask to the world so smooth, so unruffled that no one could find a chink to stick in a knife or the slightest grip to gain power over him. Ken had been on his own all his life. From now on he was going to call the shots.

Ken liked the elevator work. Sure, it was dirty, greasy, but he had a real knack for mechanics. He could figure out how things worked and how to fix them. His big hands were amazingly good at manipulating bolts and wires and gears. He had the "touch", his dad said. Unfortunately neither of them had the Midas touch. His dad hung around the downtown hotels all day, drinking, promoting business he said, coming home pissed to the eyeballs, flat broke. His dad could make money disappear like magic. He paid Ken $25 a week, when he had it. Ken paid $15 a week for a cruddy rooming house on Langside St. That left him with $10 a week spending money. It wasn't enough to buy toothpaste.

He'd been crazy to get married. Everybody told him that. Eighteen years old. No dough. How could he support a wife? It just made him stubborn. "I'll work something out," he said. He couldn't let Elva down.

Ken had met Elva in 1949 at a funeral, of all places, in Somerset, Manitoba. He'd noticed her beautiful long red hair right away. She was two years older than Ken, a big girl, fat,

his friends snickered, but Ken sort of liked that. Solid. Comfortable. Feminine. Not brittle and loud like a lot of city girls,
slathered in lipstick and greasepaint, girls who scared the
hell out of him, although he'd never admit it. Elva had pretty
soft eyes and a lovely smile. She was old-fashioned, a real
homebody. Sure, Ken should have played the field, dated a
different girl each week, screwed around, but the truth was
he couldn't afford it. City girls expected a big time, a show,
then a snack somewhere, drinks maybe, or a bottle. Ken
didn't have that kind of money. He didn't even have a car.
The girls, the nice ones anyway, would laugh at his cheap
clothes, his country manners—and he wasn't going to settle
for some dog.

Elva didn't care. Well, to tell the truth Elva didn't know.
Ken had to admit the truth got a little varnished on the way
to Somerset every Saturday morning, clinging for dear life to
the back of his friend Wally's motorcycle. Elva thought the
elevator business was a big deal, the way Ken talked. Ken
preferred to talk about the future, not the present and never
the past. The future of the elevator business was rosy, new
designs, big contracts. Ken drew Elva little pictures on the
oilcloth. Blueprints. Projections. Estimates. Elva sat quietly
and listened to his plans, making little sounds of amazement
and admiration, laughing a lot but not in a ridiculing way.
She believed in him. She loved him. It always bucked Ken
up after a tough, miserable week to see Elva's shining eyes
and bright smile. She thought he was a real wheel. Well, he
would be, pretty soon. They'd sit in the kitchen and talk and
eat. Jeez, did he eat! He fed himself pretty much for the whole
week on her cooking. It became kind of a habit, going to the
farm, a warm nest that made the rest of the week bearable,
and it seemed natural, over the year, to talk about getting
married and having kids. They both wanted a big family. Ken
didn't think he could hold off much longer. He figured he'd
have to marry her or drop her. He didn't want to hurt her,
she'd been so proud of him, and life without those weekends
seemed a cold dismal prospect, especially with Christmas
coming on.

The more Ken thought about it the more reasonable marriage seemed. They'd get a little furnished apartment some-

where. Elva would cook, he'd be able to work harder, earn more, she could get a job. Two could live as cheaply as one.

Ken put $30 down on a diamond ring at People's Credit Jewellers the day before Christmas. He was planning to pop the question Christmas Day and even had a little speech worked out. When he got to the house that night Elva was washing her hair in the kitchen sink, eyes shut, lather dripping down her bare arms. Ken impulsively slipped the ring on her wet finger. Elva shrieked with delight. Ken just stood there and grinned. It was the happiest Christmas of his life.

They set the date, February 25, 1950, two days before Elva's birthday. "I guess I'm your birthday present," Ken joked.

As the cold, black weeks of January dragged past, fingers of fear began to clutch at Ken's stomach. Business was slow; he was stone broke. Furnished apartments were scarce as hen's teeth, at least anything he could afford. He could barely scrape together the dough for a new suit, the license and the minister's fee. A month's rent would clean him out. What would he tell Elva? That she was marrying a bum, a guy who couldn't put a roof over her head? He'd look like an asshole. Anyway the invitations had gone out, the dress was finished. He couldn't back out now. Ken rented a cheap, unfurnished suite and prayed some furniture would turn up.

Late one afternoon during the last week of January Ken was cleaning an elevator in Genser's furniture warehouse on Portage Avenue. It was after five o'clock but he was anxious to finish up and start a new job in the morning. When he came up out of the shaft just before six Ken was astonished to find the offices locked and the lights out.

"Hey!" he called. "Hello? Hello?"

His voice echoed through the room. Everyone had gone home. He was locked in.

Dumbfounded, Ken stood there in the twilight and looked around. Sofas. Dressers. Tables. Beds. Lamps. Armchairs. Rugs. Acres of chrome and walnut and plastic and plush and velvet stretching as far as the eye could see, rich and dazzling as Ali Baba's cave.

Holy cow! Ken laughed out loud. How's this for luck! He walked through the warehouse, picking his way carefully among the hide-a-beds and mattresses. Here was enough furniture for the city of Winnipeg. Would they miss a single sofa? One bed? Who could blame him? It was Genser's fault.

He pushed gently on the back delivery door. It opened easily. He listened for the sound of an alarm. Nothing. The lane was deserted. Ken ran across the street to a cafe. He leafed quickly through the yellow pages at a pay phone by the door. Taxidermists. Televisions. Trucks—Delivery. He dropped a nickel into the phone.

"Hiya!" he said. "Genser's furniture calling. We got a rush order here. Going out to Virden. Transfer will pick it up tonight if we can get it to the west end right away. Can you get it to the Texaco station, Portage and Arlington, in half an hour? It's not a big load."

"Sure. Be right over."

Ken dashed back to the warehouse. He shoved an armchair over to the door. Then a sofa, a bed, spring and mattress, two end-tables, two lamps and a kitchen suite. He rearranged the remaining furniture to close the gaps.

The truck turned up in ten minutes. The driver helped Ken load the furniture.

"I'll go along to keep an eye on things." Ken said. He carefully closed the warehouse door and hopped in the truck.

"Wedding present," he winked at the driver.

The driver nodded and grinned. He helped Ken unload the furniture at the back of the service station lot. It looked weird sitting there in the snow.

"Thanks," said Ken. "Send the bill to Genser's."

He watched the truck out of sight. He went into the Texaco station and called a friend.

"Hiya, Bob? Kenny here. How are ya? Great. Look, can you help me out? I got this really great deal on some furniture this morning. Couldn't get into the apartment till tonight. Can I borrow your truck to. . . . Yeah? Terrific! Gee, that's great. Only take a sec. I'll be waiting on the corner, okay? See ya."

Ken had the furniture unloaded and neatly arranged in his apartment by seven o'clock. The place still looked pretty bare. Elva'd fix that. Wedding presents. Her hope chest. They'd need a couple more chairs, a rug. Should've taken a rug. . . . He ran his hand over the nubby nylon of the sofa. Elva'd

wonder why he hadn't taken her shopping . . . he'd tell her
he got it at an auction. That's why the sofa was green and the
chair blue. Too bad the warehouse had been so dark. . . .

There was no mention of the robbery in the papers. After
two weeks Ken stopped looking. The furniture had become
familiar. His. Why not? The Gensers were rich. The whole lot
wasn't worth $300. It had seemed the sensible thing to do
and he'd done it without really thinking. He was surprised,
later, at his nerve. He'd never thought of himself as a tough
guy, a criminal for God's sake! Ha, ha! He felt no guilt, only
excitement. The whole thing was a big joke.

"I'm probably the only guy to start his criminal career by
a break-out," he laughed to himself.

Ken and Elva were married in a quiet ceremony at her parent's
house. Elva got pregnant right away.

Early in March Ken had a chance to finish furnishing their
apartment. It was too good to miss. He hid in Genser's elevator shaft just before five o'clock. By five-thirty the place
was deserted. He selected the items he needed, a carpet, crib
and stove, and stacked them by the delivery door. He called
a truck at random from the phone book.

"Sure. Be right there."

Ken waited by the door. A big, heavy-set man appeared
in a dirty brown parka.

"You call a truck?"

"Yeah," said Ken. "Stuff's right here."

The man reached into his pocket and flashed a card.

"Police. You'd better come with me."

Before Ken knew what was happening, he was in the back
seat of a cruiser car on his way to the Rupert Street police
station. He was questioned, fingerprinted, photographed, relieved of his belt and shoelaces and locked up. He sat on his
steel bunk and cried. The police turned his apartment inside
out. Elva cried. The next day a Genser's van came and took
every stick of furniture out of the suite.

Ken pleaded guilty to both thefts. He was sentenced to nine
months in the provincial jail.

He was out in four months. In time for the birth of his
daughter, Lee Ann, in September. He went job hunting. Sorry,

Mr. Leishman, the job has been filled. We'll call you when
there's a vacancy. Try again next week. Sometimes Ken men-
tioned his record, sometimes he didn't. They found out anyway. Sorry. Nobody wanted a nineteen-year-old kid with no
education and a record. Jail, Ken realized, was a front. He
would be punished for his theft for the rest of his life. Well,
he'd show them.

His big break came in the summer of 1951. Machine Industries advertised for a young man with an agricultural back-
ground and mechanical experience to service a new line of
farm machinery. Ken landed the job.

He worked his ass off that fall, tearing over dirt roads, face
and clothes white with dust except where sweat ran in little
rivulets down his cheeks and neck, his poor old car pocked
and scratched by stones, tires worn bald, radiator steaming
up in the heat. His job was to install and service straw cutters
on combines. He enjoyed the work. Each piece of machinery
had its own quirks and idiosyncrasies, just like a person. It
was a challenge to figure them out. It gave him a real thrill
to get something working perfectly. He'd stick at it until it
was done, no matter how long it took. He actually liked the
toughest jobs best, the ones where he could think up some
new twist or gadget. Not that they always worked, but it was
fun. Ken got along with the farmers too. They were his kind
of people, practical, interested in making things work, interested in making money, that's for sure. And how they loved
to talk! On hot afternoons they knocked off to the cool gloom
of the local beer parlor and chewed the fat about the government, the price of wheat, the war, the weather, always the
weather. It was a real education for Ken, brought him out of
himself. Only the driving got him down, thirty, forty miles
between jobs over those godawful roads, wasting a whole
day, tired, impatient, farmers angry at waiting, hating the
lonely hotels at night, greasy food, weeks on the road at a
time. It didn't make sense.

"Golly," Ken said to himself. "Why don't I fly?"

Ken had never been in a plane. It cost a lot of money.
Besides, where would he go? He had no desire to travel, see
the world. But to fly his own plane! That was something else.
It would be smart business. Cover more ground, boost sales,
make more money. Worth checking out.

On a warm day in the spring of 1952 Ken was in the little shack at the Winnipeg airport that served as the office of the Winnipeg Flying Club. How much was a small aircraft? Lessons? What were the qualifications? He could hardly believe it. Thirty hours in the air and he'd be a pilot! Less than two days! Wow! A piece of cake. All he needed was a plane.

"She's for sale," The instructor nodded out the window at a tiny red aircraft parked on the tarmac. It looked as big as a dragonfly. Ken went over and looked at it. It was a two-seater Aeronea, steered with a wheel, like a car, covered in canvas. Canvas! Like something out of the first war! Billy Bishop Leishman! Ken laughed. The plane was the most beautiful thing he'd seen in his life. He took a deep breath.

"How much?"

"Owner'll take $1,000. Cheap as you'll get. Good machine to, uh, start on."

Ken figured quickly. He had enough for a down payment in the bank, he could borrow, pay on time, with extra commissions this summer he could have the plane and lessons paid for by winter.

"Sure," he said. "I'll take it."

"Okay. I'll take you up."

"Up?" Ken gulped. "Right now?"

His heart was in his mouth as they taxied down the runway, his knees around his ears. His ass felt like it was rubbing the ground. Jeez, he couldn't see a damn thing. What if they ran into something? Faster, faster, the little plane shuddering in the wind, faster, then bump, they were off the ground, weightless, climbing, flying! Ken felt like he was floating, dipping and bobbing like a cork in the ocean, the air roaring like surf in his ears. He could see forever! The houses of Winnipeg were toy boxes beneath him, doll's houses, with dinky toys in the driveways and twigs for trees. The Red and Assiniboine Rivers wound like fat earthworms through a crazy quilt of fields. As they climbed he could see Lake Winnipeg shining to the north and, to the west, yes, there it was, Headingley Jail! If they could only see him now!

Ken laughed. He had never imagined what it would be like to look down at the earth. Now he felt he'd opened his eyes for the first time, new born, a new world, a new start. All his fears and worries shrank and vanished. How tiny men were! Like ants. How silly all their schemes. Up here all was calm, serene, free. Ken felt he could stretch his arms around the world. This was what the Bible meant by Heaven!

Two weeks later Ken is sitting at the controls of the Aeronea alone, waiting for the signal to take off, his hands cold and wet with sweat. Over and over he's rehearsed the take-off procedure in his imagination. Now it's the real thing. He's heading west with a full load of machinery parts stacked in the tiny space behind his seat. He has exactly five hours of flying experience. He has no licence. This is his first solo.

There's the signal! He guns the engine. The little plane roars and trembles as it starts down the runway. Gee, it feels like it has two flat tires. Has he crammed in too much stuff? Ken opens the throttle. The plane slowly picks up speed. Faster now, faster. The grass is flying past the windows but the wheels cling to the ground. Up! Up! Ken urges, easing the wheel back. Fly! Fly! He can see the end of the runway now and the boundary fence rushing at him. It's not going to fly! He's going to crash! He feels the wheels hit the rough sod at the end of the runway. Once more he pulls back on the wheel, full throttle, fence looming up, rising out of his seat to urge the little plane over it. Fly! Fly! He's over! clearing the posts by inches, rushing towards the city now, six feet off the ground, full speed, houses ahead. Fly! Ken prays, fly! Slowly, almost imperceptibly, the Aeronea rises, gains speed, shuddering, roaring, skims the rooftops, climbs to fifty feet, a hundred, three hundred. Ken wipes his trembling hands on his pants, checks his compass and heads west.

He lands near Yorkton, Saskatchewan in a farmer's field, settling down gently on the stubble smooth as silk. He scares the farmer out of his wits.

"You all right?" The farmer runs up, waving his arms. "What the hell's goin' on?"

Ken grins. You'd think he was a man from Mars! Cars come roaring up from all directions, plumes of dust standing in the hot still air and a great crowd gathers in the farm kitchen where Ken is drinking coffee and telling how he almost didn't clear that fence, by golly. Within an hour the whole township knows about Ken, the guy with the plane full of new-fangled machinery.

Ken covered most of Saskatchewan and half of Alberta that summer. Everywhere he went the reception was the same. It's a bird! It's a plane! It's Superman! Ken would say to himself as he swooped in, buzzing the top of the farm house, scaring the bejesus out of the cows as he wafted into the pasture. He liked the pastures for landing best, then stubble, summer-fallow. He even landed on the roads, neat as a pin, keeping an eye out for telephone wires and the RCMP, who didn't appreciate an airplane speeding down a country road at eighty miles an hour. But his best trick was to come down right in the field where the farmer was swathing, settling into the eight-foot-wide cut between the swaths and taxiing right up to the machine without disturbing a single grain. Knocked their eyes out.

Ken often took people up for joy rides, twenty-five cents a trip. They were so excited! He'd show off sometimes too, doing loops and stalls over a country school house while all the kids stood outside and gawked. You'd think he was a whole circus! Well, it was nice to bring some excitement into their lives. Good business too.

Ken was making big plans for next summer when he finally headed back to Winnipeg in September.

He was nailed for flying without a licence. The maximum penalty was one year in jail or a $5,000 fine. He got off with a suspended sentence.

Machine Industries closed down. The factory, an old hangar near the airport, had been sold to Bristol Aerospace for the manufacture of CF-100 fighter planes. Ken was offered a good job supervising an assembly line. He jumped at it. This was it! He pictured himself at a drafting board, drawing plans, flying around the world faster than speed of sound. He'd been on the job six weeks when he was summoned to the manager's office. The manager was polite but grave. Sensitive defence contracts. RCMP. Routine security check. Ken felt the world slipping away from under his feet. His record. Regulations. Have to let him go. Sorry. Ken turned and fled.

He sat in a bar for hours nursing a single stale drink. His heart was hard and his body stiff with anger. So that was it, eh? No matter how hard he worked, no matter how smart he was, how honest, he'd always be a crook. All for a bunch of crummy furniture! It would be better to hang people and be done with it.

Well, to hell with them! He was young, strong. He could get along. He wasn't going to beg, kiss ass, apologize for being alive. Not him. You slap some people down, they break. Not Ken. The harder he got slapped the tougher, prouder, sharper he got, like tempered steel. He'd done his time, paid his debt. Jeez, you'd think he was a maniac, a murderer or something. All he wanted was a fair shake. A chance to get ahead. Well, from now on he'd go his own way. Screw 'em. He'd show them.

YOU
CAN EARN
up to
$10,000 a YEAR!!!!!!
Drive a Cadillac! Work on your own time!
In your own home! Be your own boss!

A New Company
is looking for
BRIGHT CONFIDENT KEEN
SALESMEN
for a new luxury line!
Bonuses! Fast Promotion! Free training!

It was a big ad that caught Ken's eye right away. Looked phony. Only rich guys drove Caddies. A real come on. Sucker bait. He'd never sold anything in his life . . . . Ken pondered the ad for a long time. He was twenty-three, out of work, in debt. A fourth baby was on the way. What the hell. He couldn't be choosy. He'd try anything once.

The luxury line turned out to be pots and pans, or stainless steel cookware, as the manager reverently called it. The manager was an old school friend of Ken's from Treherne. Ken was in like Flynn. No questions asked. He'd get sales training, a kit, a territory and he'd be on his own. Straight commission. Cookware was selling like hotcakes. Top men were making $1,000 a month. Minimum.

Ken jumped at it. He had it figured right away. He'd back-track his old farm machinery route. He knew hundreds of people out there, a lot of them still cooking on wood stoves, no electricity, where would they buy stuff like this, miles from a big store? They'd love it! Who cared more about food than farmers? Nobody! Who spent more time in the kitchen? Nobody! He'd bring the stuff right to their front doors, $200 a set. Cash. He'd fly out in the fall when the grain cheques were coming in. . . .

In the last warm days of August, when the combines were roaring through the golden fields, Ken once more wafted out of the sky onto the Saskatchewan stubble with his load of pots and pans, practical, efficient, high quality, last a lifetime, a real bargain, a good investment. He had his pitch down pat but people were so dazzled by his plane, a new three-seater Stinson with "Queen Anne" emblazoned on the side in foot-high letters, so taken by this tall young man with the big brown eyes and soft, mellow voice, so excited by the adventure that Ken could have sold six hundred pairs of woolly red long-johns if that's what he'd had on board. He sold pots and pans hand over fist, word spreading like wildfire so if he made one sale in a community he usually made a dozen. He even sold four whole sets to a Hutterite colony. Pre-paid. Cash. He was the superman of stainless steel.

Ken was promoted to supervisor, then manager for Saskatchewan, entitled to a cut of other salesmen's commissions. That Christmas he was the second-best salesman in the company. He lost out on a free TV by a single sale. His prize was a clothes dryer. Elva was thrilled.

Ken made a lot of money, more than $10,000 a year, not a fortune, but pretty damn good for a twenty-five-year-old. He bought his Cadillac. He owned two planes. Dressed well. Spent lavishly. Presents. Drinks for his buddies. Steaks at the Town n' Country restaurant. He was a high flier. Some people said he was a fly-by-night con artist. The cookware business had a bad reputation. Salesmen cheating. Ripping off the old age pensioners, widows. Screwing the customers. Literally.

Ken didn't feel there was anything sleazy about what he was doing. Sure, it was hard sell, but it was a service too. His customers weren't children. He wasn't forcing them to buy anything. It was a contest of wits and wills. Ken usually won.

He was good at selling. Really good. He loved the pressure, the risk, the emotional drain. It gave him a real kick, got the adrenalin pumping until he kind of took off, brain whirring like a propeller, working twelve, eighteen hours a day, hardly stopping to sleep or eat, thinking up new gambits, new deals, new products. But it was more than just work. Ken mastered the art of selling as quickly as he'd learned to fly. He had a gift for it. He'd always been friendly, eager to please, sensitive, vulnerable, hungry for affection. Rebuffs, cruelty always hurt him. He was a snail without a shell. The sales training gave him an instant shell that he put on as readily and happily as a new suit of clothes. He learned good manners, how to be polite, courteous in every situation. One curse, one angry word was a lost sale. He learned how to flatter people with his attention, look them straight in the eye, maintain that eye contact no matter what he was doing, rummaging in his kit, drinking coffee, break it only after the sale was closed. He'd always studied men he admired, important men, bankers, managers, cops, even the judge who sent him to jail, now *there* was power! He could tell the big guns by the way they moved, slowly, quietly, stern faces, deep voices. They radiated authority, control. Ken taught himself to move that way, deliberately, gracefully, in a way that attracted attention to himself. He spoke softly so people had to listen to what he was saying. He used big words even when he didn't understand what they meant. He wore dark, conservative clothes that made him look older, even old-fashioned, and carried snapshots of Elva and the kids in his breast pocket. He didn't smoke, drink or swear in public. He liked sports, especially baseball and hockey, kids, country music, Rosemary Clooney and Doris Day—although his favourite song was "The Wayward Wind" by Gogi Grant. He hated rock and roll. He loved to tell jokes, dirty ones when the ladies weren't around, although when he was working a shower party he found a little tongue-in-cheek smut usually got the girls excited.

Women loved Ken. He liked them. He liked to sit over a coffee and shoot the breeze. He liked to cook. Ken always cooked the meat when he was home, steaks, roasts, only the best, he'd had enough salt pork and blood sausage as a kid. Ugh. He often gave out his super recipe for steak sauce: one cup catsup, two cups water, one tablespoon tabasco sauce, one ounce vinegar, one teaspoon garlic and half a cup of brown sugar. "Dad's Sauce," his kids called it. Ken really knew his pots and pans. He had a "feel" for people too, an intuitive way of tuning in on their emotions, putting them at ease, making them laugh, like when he whipped a big red silk handkerchief out of his pocket and let it drift to the floor, a magic carpet to show off his wares. He never seemed tense or scary the way a lot of salesmen were, but always calm, relaxed, easy going. He was sexy, funny, charming, the dark stranger the fortune teller had promised, mysterious, dangerous, yet sympathetic, innocent. Beneath his suave, cocky manner Ken retained a touching naiveté, a slightly bewildered attitude to life, as if it were a tricky piece of machinery, an elevator perhaps, which might run out of control at any minute. He never seemed to grasp the grubby machinations of everyday life, the drudgery, compromises, modest joys. He remained a child in his limitless enthusiasms, optimisms, expectations, the crushing grief of his disappointments.

Ken was disappointed in the fall of 1957. Queen Anne had gone out of business, bang, just like that. He was stuck in the middle of his peak season, no money, no work, and tired. Gosh, he was tired! Most guys burned out after a year. He'd been knocking around for more than ten years. Where was he going to be in another ten? Flogging his ass around the country like a tinker? He was a family man now. He had responsibilities, a reputation as a successful businessman, a go-getter, a mover. What if he lost that? Went broke? Who'd ever hire him again?

He thought about suicide. He thought about running away, flying to Mexico or South America, starting over with a new name, a new life. Everywhere around him he saw men with good steady jobs, houses, security, respect, even fame, stupid men a lot of them, dull, crooked. Why couldn't he get ahead? Honesty didn't have much to do with it, that's for sure. Everyone lied, cheated, swindled. If you did it on a big enough scale you were a pillar of the community.

Panic ate away at Ken's self-control, sucked at his strength. He had headaches, nightmares about being in jail, waking to the dull clang of the bars. That's all he was. A crook. A thief. Why pretend? Face it. Okay. This time he wouldn't get caught.

The idea for the bank robbery came to Ken in a dream so vivid he woke up with a jump, thinking he'd already done it. He knew exactly what he would wear and what he would say, even what the manager would say. The vision was so real it took on the force of inevitability. Everything had been planned out for him. It seemed the sensible thing to do. Banks had money; he needed money. Simple. Ken's fear fell away from him. He was calm and composed and perfectly confident. And he'd pulled it off, the first time, a perfect score. Even in Stony Mountain, after his capture, he still relived it. Was that really him? How had he done it? If only he'd taken the whole wad. . . . Next time he'd go for the really big bucks. Next time.

CHAPTER
THREE

Goldfinger

KEN WASN'T IN STONY MOUNTAIN an hour before he was planning to get out. There were two ways, he learned: the quick way, over the wall, and the slow way, parole.

He tried the quick way first. He'd been given a good job, stringing electric lights around the outdoor hockey rink so they could play after supper. He figured that if he could get out on some pretext, after dark, he might have a chance to scale the wall. He made arrangements through a lawyer for a buddy to be waiting for him in a car down the road from the prison with a change of clothes in a suitcase and $2,000 cash. The lawyer would have his aircraft warmed up for him at the airport. He'd head south. Cuba maybe. But things went wrong. Somebody squealed. The night Ken was planning to go, all the floodlights were turned on around the prison grounds. Jeez, it was bright as day! He didn't have a chance. He denied the whole thing, said he'd been framed, but he got ten days in the hole anyway. It made him a hero in the pen.

He decided to try parole. Parole was a tricky business. It depended on a lot of things: good behaviour, job prospects, family stability, the convict's personality and state of mind, the opinion of social workers, the warden's recommendation, political pressure, the whim of the parole board. Ken studied the parole regulations with the same single-minded concentration he brought to everything. He had a little help too, from a friend of his in Stony, a lawyer, mousy little guy, doing time for embezzling a hundred grand of his clients' money. Now that was class! Ken could learn a lot from him. Who could beat the system better than a lawyer?

Ken became a model prisoner. Gee, butter wouldn't melt in his mouth! No matter how angry, upset or sad he was he always put on a happy face. Cheerful, cooperative, that was him! He worked hard at whatever crappy job they gave him. He enrolled in two high school correspondence courses and studied every night until the lights went out. He joined the debating club. He took a Dale Carnegie course on How to Win Friends and Influence People. He refereed hockey and baseball games. He acted in the drama club. He listened patiently to other prisoners' complaints, championed their grievances, wrote their letters. He edited the prison newspaper, *Mountain Echoes*, and wrote most of the copy himself, even the poems:

    The sun is past, long shadows cast,
    God's creatures pause to rest.
    As night descends, day's clamour ends
    And tiny tots are blessed.
    Now little feet depart the street
    And mighty wars are stilled
    Each little man a hero grand,
    A thousand bad men killed.
    As night draws nigh, each Mom will sigh
    Content to pause and rest,
    Since early sun her young have run
    In never-ending quest.
    Throughout the day what Mom won't say
    She ran a dozen miles
    Restoring bliss, a bruise to kiss
    That turns big tears to smiles.
    Now off to bed you sleepy-head
    With teddy bear held tight,
    A kiss, a hug, a sleepy shrug
    Sweet dreams invade the night.

It wasn't long before Ken was king of the rock. He was older than most of the cons. They called him "dad" because of his bald head, but always with respect. They admired his brains, his style; they went to him for advice. He remained aloof, dignified, cherishing the distance that separated him from the prison goons who ran Stony with a combination of bribery, rape and terror. Ken worked out in the gym and bragged about the guys he'd flattened, but he knew his big fists would be no protection against a knife. Guys were killed all the time. His best defence was superiority of intellect, personality, will power. He practiced self-discipline. He learned control.

The guards liked Ken. The warden liked Ken. Here was a guy they could talk to, reason with, a friendly guy, gentle, seemed too bad. . . . Ken was given jobs he liked, in the kitchen, in charge of the prison library. He didn't mind the routine, it wasn't much worse than the army, he figured, and he was flattered by his prestige, the attention of the young cons. He felt sorry for them, some of them were so dumb, so mixed up, never had a chance, just kids really.

Ken tried not to think about his own kids. Five of them now, four boys. How he missed them! He loved to wrestle with them on the living room floor, letting them all pile on at once, screaming and tickling, playing horsey or big brown bear. Ken liked to give the kids their baths and feed them, and in the summer he took them to the park to play catch or see the zoo. Sure, it was a big responsibility, five little kids, sometimes it seemed that Elva got pregnant every time he looked at her, but he wouldn't have traded his kids for the world. He lived for his family. He wanted them to have everything he never had as a kid. That's why he'd worked so hard, gotten so desperate, so his kids could have a better life. How he wished he could see them, hold them, just for a second. Were they sick? Cold? Hungry? Sad? If only he could pick up the phone. . . . And Elva. What was she doing? Dancing? Drinking? Screwing some guy . . .? It almost drove Ken nuts, not knowing, imagining, not that he could really blame her. Why should she stick by him? She'd be better off to find some rich guy, raise the kids decently, he'd been a rotten husband, she owed him nothing. It would be better to cut himself off from his family, go his own way, day by day, like the other guys in the pen, not be torn apart by worry, fear. Cut them out of his mind, his heart.

He was afraid he'd break down, lose control, turn into an animal like the other guys. That's what they were, animals in cages. Often at night one of them would start to roar, howl, bang his head against the bars, the screams echoing up and down the tiers, reverberating from the stone walls around and around until another voice joined in, and another, yelling, bellowing until the whole prison was shaking with the sound of bone against steel, the crash of breaking glass, smashing toilet bowls, chairs, desks, mattresses torn apart by bare hands, feathers floating down like snow, the terrible symphony trailing off at last into a chorus of racking sobs while Ken, frozen with horror, would huddle in the corner of his cell, silent.

At first Elva wrote every day and visited once a month. Then the letters began to dwindle. Three a week, two, sometimes none. Ken heard rumours. Boyfriends. Her parents trying to split them up. Elva didn't write for two months, then started again, but her letters seemed evasive, trivial. Ken peppered her with letters. What was the matter? Had he said something? What could he do to patch things up? He asked questions, made accusations, demanded answers, invented rumours, stories that seemed almost crazy. Elva ignored his letters. She stopped writing altogether. Ken wrote his mom. Would she speak to Elva? Find out the truth. He asked ministers to visit. Social workers. The Salvation Army. Ken became like a man possessed. Prison was destroying his marriage, his family, his sanity. Is that what they wanted? He fought back, desperately marshalling all his skills as a supersalesman to sell his most valuable product—himself.

He wrote to lawyers. He wrote the magistrate who sentenced him, suggesting a reduction in his term. He wrote the parole board. He wrote his mom, his sister, his friends, asking them to plead on his behalf. He wrote to politicians demanding an investigation of the penal system. Ken's letters were shaky on grammar but passionate, well-reasoned and persuasive. He made a host of important contacts and some influential friends. Social worker Ken Howard gained Elva's confidence and patched the marriage together.

Elva had sold the house and bought a restaurant on Portage Avenue with living quarters above. It was just a small place, a lunch counter, but it was a tough grind, opening up early for the coffee crowd and staying open late, looking after a new baby, the little kids underfoot, doing the cooking and the cleaning up, trying to balance the books. She was worn out, discouraged. With Howard's encouragement, Elva quit her job, went on welfare and waited for Ken to get out. The family, Ken knew, was his ace, his ticket to freedom. He was no bum! He was a devoted husband, a loving father, a successful businessman, smart, hard-working, decent, gentle, a nice guy trying to get ahead. He'd made a mistake. Jeez, he was sorry!

The parole board bought the new, reformed Ken Leishman. Ken was released on parole the day before Christmas, 1961. He'd served forty-four months of his twelve year sentence.

One of the friends Ken had made in Stony was a lawyer, Harry Backlin. Harry'd been a law student at the University of Manitoba. He'd come out to the pen as part of a debating team shortly after Ken got there. Ken remembered the topic of the debate: Is there one law for the rich and another for the poor? He'd taken to Harry right away. Harry was a big, easy-going, friendly guy, a little older than Ken, from the country, like Ken, full of hustle, big ideas. Harry helped Ken land a job, in sales, after his release. He sort of took Ken under his wing, introduced him to people, invited him and Elva up to the house, represented Ken in a suit to recover some lost wages from the cookware company. Ken was grateful, flattered. Harry was a good guy to know.

A couple of days after Christmas, 1965, Ken is splitting a bottle of Christmas cheer with Harry and a couple of business partners in the darkened office of the Olgat Corporation near the Winnipeg airport. No one is cheerful. Olgat, a manufacturer of cleaning products, is bankrupt. It's bad news for Ken. He'd been promised the job of general manager. He could use it too. He's been knocking around for four years, selling, not really getting anywhere. He'd hoped to start a company making prefab steel buildings but that hadn't panned out. Now he's into cosmetics, a new line of organic products, made from lettuce, strawberries and stuff, high class, expensive, mixed up to suit each woman's hair and skin by a team of trained cosmeticians. It had seemed a sure fire idea, like Avon, selling in the privacy of a woman's home, free samples, free facials, exclusive products, so he'd gone into it in a really big way, figuring he'd clean up in the Christmas rush. What a dope he'd been! At Christmas people bought gifts. His stuff couldn't be given away because it depended on individual analysis. Sales had been nowhere. Jeez, it seemed like his whole house was full of lipsticks and face powder!

"We need a gold mine," laughs Harry bleakly.

"We can always hold up the plane," jokes a partner.

"What plane?"

"Transair. Flies gold bricks in from the mine at Red Lake, Ontario, once, twice a month. Goes to the mint. Ottawa. Pure gold. Millions."

"Pussy Galore!" laughs Ken. He's tense now, listening. He waits for the guffaws to die down before he pushes. Where does the gold go? How is it shipped? Is it guarded?

"You kiddin'?" scoffs the partner. "Fort Knox. Three, four RCMP. Armoured car. Not a chance."

Ken lies awake that night. Thinking. Excitement tickling his brain. He's thought about gold a lot in the eight years since he was building his lodge up north. The Indians there told a story about a tractor train loaded with gold that had gone through the ice on Island Lake. Sunk like a stone. Never found. An old trapper had seen the hole. Knew where it was. All it would take would be a couple of scuba divers, a rig to haul the gold to the surface. . . . He'd tucked the story away in the back of his mind. If only he could swim. . . .

Ken phones Transair the next morning. Yes, one flight a day from Red Lake, arriving Winnipeg at 10 p.m.

Ken is at the airport that night at 9:55 p.m. It's cold enough to freeze a witch's tit! He's a damn fool running around on these wild goose chases. He should go home, stick to the straight and narrow. He fights with himself, pacing around with the handful of people waiting for the flight beside the baggage carousel near gate 1A. Transair always uses this gate at the extreme northern end of the Winnipeg terminal, parking its old DC3s on the edge of the tarmac near the fence. Ken notices that it's very dark out there beyond the circle of flood-lights.

The flight comes in on time. Ken watches a member of the ground crew push the steps up to the door. The passengers file out. The baggage attendant drives a buggy up under the belly of the plane, unlocks the hold and throws out suitcases. The steps are wheeled away. The plane slowly taxis to the edge of the tarmac and kills its lights.

Heck! Ken scowls. Not much to that. Unless they put the gold in a suitcase. Not bloody likely. He'd read up on gold that afternoon in the library. You didn't just throw it around, that's for sure! He's learned a lot about gold. How is he going to find out what flight the gold is on, if it's on? He can't hang around here every night. Asking questions might arouse suspicion. . . .

Ken wanders into the dinky little Transair freight office just after 9:30 p.m. the next day. The agent is a young guy, brand new uniform, neat desk, just a kid really.

"Hiya!" says Ken, sticking out his big hand. "Got a business deal on the go and need a little advice. You look like a guy with expertise!"

The agent flushes.

"Dunno," he mumbles. "Only been here a couple of months. Can I help you?"

"I'd appreciate it if you'd treat this conversation in confidence, Mr. . . ."

"Waters. Chuck."

"Good to know ya, Chuck. Listen, you know how business is. Don't want someone stealin' my pants before I get 'em on!"

"Sure."

"Well, there's a lot of development goin' on in the north, I'm sure you know, mining, hydro, going to be really big up there in the next few years, look at Thompson, so I figure there'll be a real future in the air freight business, not that I want to cut you guys out, just service those places that aren't economical for a big operation like yours. Just a one man show to start with, single plane, but she'd have to be a good one, you know what I mean. Now I have my eye on the old DC3 . . . ."

The agent sits up, interested. He launches into a long, detailed discussion of the freight capacities of the Transair planes, their idiosyncrasies, defects, suitability for the north.

"Hey!" he starts up, looking at his watch. "Red Lake's coming in right now. We'll take a look."

Ken follows him up the stairs and out on the tarmac. The passengers are already coming off. The baggage hold is open. Ken strolls over for a look.

"Just a sec!" The agent runs up the steps. The stewardess hands him a canvas pouch. Ken watches him extract some papers, scribble a signature. He clatters back down.

"Okeydoke!" He motions Ken towards the nose of the plane where an attendant is opening a hatch.

"Heavy freight's up here." He points to a conveyor belt groaning into action. "You can have a look when we've unloaded."

The belt begins to hum and a small wooden box slides out of the hold. Ken figures it's a little more than a foot long, about eight inches wide and six high. It's bound with metal straps and carries a big red seal. The attendant swears as he lifts it on to the dolly. Saliva begins to collect in the back of Ken's throat.

A second box slips out of the plane. A third. A fourth.

"How many more of these buggers?" calls the attendant. He's an older man, in his fifties Ken figures, wiry, pretty strong. It takes all his strength to lift a single box. Ken thinks fast. How much can he lift? Eighty, hundred pounds? Discount the guy's age, size, one of these boxes must be sixty, seventy pounds. Say seventy pounds of gold at $35 an ounce, that's about $30,000, $180,000 for six bars, double that on the black market.

"Is that what you call swinging lead?" Ken laughs.

"Naw!" The attendant snorts. "It's goldbrickin'! Ha, ha!"

"That's got it," says the agent as the fifth box slides down the belt. The attendant climbs on the dolly, guns the motor and tootles off down the tarmac towards the south end of the terminal.

Ken spends ten minutes inspecting the empty hold of the DC3. He apologizes to the agent for keeping him late.

"I'll keep in touch," he says. "If things get off the ground I'll need a manager. Maybe we can talk it over. If it takes off, who knows how big it'll get."

"Great," says Chuck. "Come by any time."

Ken walks towards the parking lot at the south end of the terminal. He slides into his stationwagon, starts the engine and sits for five minutes. Getting on for 11 p.m. He slips out and darts in the south entrance to the terminal, down the basement and through a door marked Air Canada—Freight Office.

"Hiya!" he says, sticking out his hand. "Expecting a parcel today from Edmonton. Any sign of it? Name's Anderson, Bill Anderson."

The agent bends and leafs through a stack of waybills.

"Jeez!" says Ken. "If that bugger's missed the flight I'm really up the creek, let me tell you!" He keeps up a running patter while his eyes rapidly scan the room.

He can hardly miss the cop. There he is big as life right at the desk beside the agent, not RCMP as Ken had expected but a rent-a-cop, an elderly man in a dark blue uniform. Gun. And behind him, in a wire cage, is the gold.

The agent searches diligently through piles of packages in the office. Ken trades jokes with the cop.

"Gee, thanks, Mr. uh . . . ." Ken says finally.

"Blair. John Blair."

"Mr. Blair. Really appreciate it."

"It might come in on the 3:35 a.m. flight. If you try in the morning . . . ."

"Gee, thanks!" says Ken. "Great idea!"

Ken is back at 8:30 a.m. the next day. The cop is gone. The gold is gone. There is no package for Mr. Anderson.

"You're nuts!" Harry says when Ken tells him his plan. "How are you gonna get rid of gold bricks? Eh? Take 'em to the Safeway to pay the grocery bill? Sorry ma'am, don't have anything smaller. Ha, ha!"

"Harry," Ken explains patiently. "You know how big a grand of pure gold is? Like a pat of butter. You can carry it in your shoe. Under your belt. You can go to Chicago. San Francisco. You don't sell it all at once. A little at a time. How long do you think a whole planeload would last? A lifetime, Harry, a lifetime."

"You get nailed, Kenny, and you'll get life all right. Life in Stony."

Ken doesn't sell much makeup in January. It's one of the coldest winters Winnipeg can remember, day after day at forty, forty-five below. The housewives Ken's recruited as cosmeticians won't go out the door. Once more he faces bankruptcy.

Ken hangs around the Winnipeg airport. The guys in the control tower are surprised to see him at first. "I thought you were in the clink!" one of them blurts, looking like he'd seen a ghost. But after a couple of evenings they get used to him. It's slow on the graveyard shift and Ken's good company. He describes his crimes in full, lurid detail, no embarrassment, a big joke on himself. He's thick-skinned now, layers of scar tissue, tough, cynical. Johnny Straight-Arrow now, he says, has an office a few blocks away, likes to drop over after work, talk flying, might buy a plane again some day. Ken spends a lot of time in the Transair freight office, hangs around the bar, the coffee shop. He learns a lot of interesting things about the Winnipeg air terminal.

No cops in sight. No armoured car.

No one but Transair personnel can see the aircraft as it's unloaded.

No flights come in or depart at the same time as Transair 108 from Red Lake.

Nobody at Air Canada gives a shit about anything. Turnover is so great the guys don't even know each other's names. And care less.

Ken checks everywhere for hidden cameras, bugs, alarms, peepholes. Nothing. He can't believe it. Air Canada offices are deserted at coffee break. Ken helps himself to a waybill, taking it carefully from the middle of the pile. He finds that the Air Canada freight truck, a white GMC van, is kept in a deserted hangar overnight, keys in the ignition. He walks in one night, starts the engine, drives out and down the tarmac towards Gate 1A, stops, turns around and drives back. He parks the car and closes the door. No one has paid the slightest attention.

Ken needs help. He's always worked alone. But he can't do this one alone. It makes him nervous. Partners will have to know what's in the boxes. They'll want a slice of the action. What if they blab? He knows of a couple of guys in Montreal,

real pros, no, he wants guys who are clean, no records, ordinary guys you'd never dream would pull a job like this.

Like Harry. Smart. Respectable.

"You don't have to lift a finger, Harry!" Ken says. "Just make a little 'business trip.' Set up a deal, bait the hook. They'll do the rest. Safe as a church. Fifty-fifty split."

"On the works?"

"The works."

"Show me the stuff and I'll think about it."

Harry applies for a passport. His wife is pushing for a trip to Acapulco. He might need it. You never know. Ken applies too. Sure, he's still on parole, four years left in his sentence, but it's worth a try. Ken gives Harry's name as a character witness. Harry gives Ken's name.

To pull the job Ken needs a couple of young fellows, hustlers, lots of nerve, guys like he'd been ten years ago. High fliers.

John Berry is twenty-six, sharp, good-looking, a Nova Scotia bluenose with a taste for fast cars, fast women and high living. Ken hired Berry a couple of years back as a cookware salesman. Now Berry's into Tupperware, working out of Calgary. Like Ken, he's always broke.

"Holy shit!" Berry whistles when Ken lays the plan on him over a beer in the Black Knight room of the Airport Hotel.

"Think of it as the biggest sale of your life," urges Ken. "Two grand in commission. Ten minutes work."

"You really serious?" asks Berry.

"Look," says Ken intensely. "It's just waiting for us. We pick it up right off the plane and drive away. Salt it away two, three years and unload it ounce by ounce. Of course, if you're chicken I'll get someone else. . . ."

"Hold it. I'll look it over."

Berry figures he'll need a partner. Ken agrees to put out another $2,000.

"I've got just the guy," says John. "Ricky Grenkow. His old man's a dentist. We can say the stuff's for fillings. Ha, ha!"

Rick Grenkow is twenty-four. He's sold pots and pans for John Berry, working the Ukrainian areas of northwestern Manitoba where his family had homesteaded. Rick's father

is one of Winnipeg's most respected dentists, one of the first
Ukrainians to make it in a traditionally WASP profession.
Rick has gone to university, dropped a couple of courses, lost
interest. His main interests in January, 1966, are money, girls
and clothes. Rick is a flashy dresser, at least the first thing
you notice about Ricky Grenkow is his clothes, his immaculate dark suit, white shirt, bright tie and shiny cowboy boots
with pointed toes and thick soles to make him appear taller.
It's an odd garb for a kid in 1966, when everybody's getting
into denim and beads, but it's not Rick's clothes so much as
his pride in them that attracts attention. He's as neat, pressed,
lint-free as an Eaton's mannequin. Rick interprets attention
as admiration, specially the attention of neat chicks. Rick
brags that his appeal is so fatal he can hypnotize any bimbo
he sets his dark eye on. Mothers scream when they see him
coming, he says. Their daughters' virtue is gone for good.
Ricky talks big. He acts big. So when John Berry hits him
with the idea of lifting a million bucks in gold from Transair
Rick gulps once and says "Sure."

Ken has maps of the airport, plans of the terminal, street
maps of the surrounding area. During February John and
Rick go over them again and again in the Olgat warehouse.
At nine o'clock they knock off for a couple of beers in the
Black Knight room, play a little shuffleboard, then, about 9:45
p.m., drive over to the airport to watch Transair 108 come in
from Red Lake. They drive the escape route over and over
until they have the time down to five minutes.

One night in the middle of February Ken turns up with
two huge pairs of white painter's coveralls and two navy blue
parkas that he'd picked up at the Army and Navy Surplus
Store. John and Rick practice scrambling into the coveralls
fully clothed, cowboy boots and all, and scrambling out again.
The transformation is startling. With parka hoods up they
look exactly like Air Canada ground crew. Ken cuts an Air
Canada logo off a cardboard box. He stencils it on the parkas
with red ink.

That night John and Rick steal the Air Canada truck and
drive it towards the Transair gate just as flight 108 is arriving.
They park and wait. Three boxes of gold come down the belt.
Rick wants to go for it. Uh, uh, says John. Ken won't move
for less than $100,000. They drive back. No one notices.

Gold has come in February 1 and February 16. Ken figures March 1 is next. This is it. He's out of cash. God, those boys could drink! Ken had never seen anything like it, beer, whiskey, homebrew, you name it. They're restless, losing their edge, goofing off. Ken's saleman's sense of timing tells him the moment to close has come.

"I need a little seed money," Ken tells Harry on February 17. "Look on it as an investment."

"I'm going on holiday," says Harry. "Two weeks. Mexico."

"That's fine," says Ken. "Perfect alibi. You don't have to lay a finger on the stuff, Harry."

"How much do you want?"

"Four grand."

"Shit! You think I'm a millionaire?"

"Two grand then. Two more when the stuff's delivered."

"Shit."

"Think of the stakes, Harry."

Ken feels a little queasy about Harry. What if he doesn't play along? Turns him in? No, Ken says, pushing his fear away. Harry'll come through.

Ken's passport arrives on February 28. A good omen. Everything's set. It will be the biggest theft in Canadian history. The crime of the century.

March 1, 1966; 9 p.m.

"Let's go!" Ken dashes into the Olgat warehouse. "It's a real payload!"

John and Rick are sitting around a flashlight in the darkened warehouse splitting a bottle. The power and telephone have been cut off. A perfect hideout.

"Paul counted 'em," Ken crows. "Twelve little babies sitting outside the Red Lake office. Paul says he could've picked one up and walked off with it under his arm!"

Paul Grenkow, Rick's older brother, is the fifth man on the job. Paul has been in Red Lake for two weeks selling vacuum cleaners. Every night he's driven out to the airport after eight o'clock looking, so he's said, for a package from Winnipeg. He's inspected the freight racks outside the Transair office door. Tonight, on the rack reserved for outgoing freight to Winnipeg, he's seen what he's been looking for: five rectangular wooden boxes, strapped and sealed. His heart sank at first. Only five. Hardly worth it. He'd been ready to leave when a taxi drove up, a uniformed guard hopped out, flipped open the trunk and heaved out seven more boxes.

Paul drove into Red Lake very slowly, not to attract attention.

"It's a boy!" he'd said to Ken on the phone. "Twelve pounds."

"Great news!" Ken had said. "Gee. Congratulations!"

Elva had said it was the biggest baby she'd ever heard of.

Ken, John and Rick drive the two blocks to the Black Knight room, order their usual six draft, play their usual game of shuffleboard and leave at 9:30 p.m. Ken checks his watch.

"See you in an hour." He climbs into his beat up Chrysler stationwagon and drives off. Ken parks beside the Olgat warehouse, goes in, and waits.

John and Rick speed towards the airport in John's white Ford Galaxie convertible. The icy roads are deserted.

"Take it easy, Berry," says Rick. "We don't want fuzz on our tail."

"They can't see it," laughs John. "I cut the tail-lights."

It's a windy night, black, about five below, smells of snow. Berry kills his headlights as they near the Transair headquarters building, an ugly, squat box about a quarter mile southeast of the terminal. The car pulls around back into the parking lot.

"Holy shit!" Berry spits between his teeth. A strange white station wagon is parked beside the Transair building and a shaft of light shows between the curtains in one of the ground floor windows.

"Christ," says Rick. "Trust some asshole to work late tonight! Christ, Ken'll kill us. . . ."

"Shut up." Berry turns off the ignition. They wait in the shadows at the back of the lot. One minute. Two. The light doesn't flicker. No one comes out. Nine-fifty.

"Let's go," says John.

In the shadow of a snowdrift they struggle into their white coveralls and blue parkas, pull up the hoods, slip on thin kid gloves. Then they run, slipping and sliding in their cowboy boots, towards the Air Canada hangar.

The back door is open. John goes in. Rick runs around the front ready to open the sliding metal door.

John peers into the gloom. There it is, a white shape near the wall. He's climbing into the cab when he hears a noise behind him. Rick? He wheels around. A figure in a parka is silhouetted in the open door.

"Anybody here?" calls a hesitant voice.

John swallows hard. He strains his eyes through the darkness. The man walks towards the truck. An older man, stooped, walks slowly, not a cop.

"Air Canada," says John, surprised at how calm his voice sounds. "Working overtime tonight."

"Oh." The man pauses for a moment, looks about. "You haven't seen the *Toronto Telegram*, have you?"

"Eh?"

"The commissary says it's here. Don't know why they'd want it. Day-old paper."

"No, sorry." John guns the engine.

"I'll get the door for you." The man shuffles off towards the sliding metal door.

"Gee, thanks!" John calls after him. He wheels the truck around as the door clatters open.

"Close it behind me, will ya?" he calls as he drives out. "Thanks a million!"

Rick runs over and climbs in.

"Who the hell was that?"

"Just a friend." John hoots with laughter.

He drives across the tarmac and stops under the observation deck just in front of gate 5. Transair 108 is taxiing in, right on time, about a hundred yards ahead.

Rick is sweating in his heavy parka but he feels stark naked sitting out there under the floodlights. His glasses are fogged and his hands are numb with cold. He puts them in his pockets, fingering the waybill. Wait, Ken said. Wait until you see the boxes coming off. Don't rush it. Timing. You don't want to stand around, giving people time to ask questions, time to think. You move right in, close the deal and scram.

Rick takes a pull from his pocket mickey.

The passengers are coming down the steps.

"Want a smoke?" John holds out a pack of Craven As.

"Naw."

John inhales in long, slow drags. Now the Transair dolly is driving up to the plane. He watches Chuck Waters disappear up the ladder into the open door. The cargo hatch opens. The first wooden box jerks slowly down the conveyor belt. A second. A third.

"Away we go!" John drives quickly up to the plane, right under the nose, wheels the truck around and backs up to the dolly. The truck neatly blocks the light from the terminal. John and Rick jump out. Rick opens the back doors on the truck.

"Got a rush order tonight," John says to the attendant heaving the fourth gold bar on to the dolly. "Save you guys some work."

Rick holds out the waybill.

Glen Shrimpton glances at it, straightens up, wipes his forehead on the sleeve of his jacket, runs his fingers through his curly blond hair. Shrimpton's a husky guy, strong, thickset. He's been with Transair ten years and he figures he's getting a little old, at thirty-five, to be heaving freight around. Time he got a promotion, snazzy uniform, cushy desk job like that kid, Chuck Waters. He's not going to turn up his nose at a little help.

"Suits me," he shrugs. "You'll have to see the boss. Hey, Chuck!"

John Berry lifts a wooden box from the dolly. Holy Shit! The goddamn thing weighs a ton! He staggers over to the truck and dumps it in the back. Shrimpton laughs. Lazy bastards, the Air Canada guys, he figures. Never lift a finger.

"You buggers out of shape?" he taunts. "Here. Lemme give you a hand."

Shrimpton picks up a second box and dumps it in the back of the truck.

Chuck Waters scrambles out of the plane, a sheaf of papers in his hand, just like Ken said.

"What's up?"

"Late flight leaving in half-an-hour," says Rick, holding out his waybill. "Ottawa wants this stuff right away. Must've run out, I guess. Ha, ha!"

Chuck Waters is puzzled. He's never done it this way before. Trust the government. Always screwing things around.

He looks at the waybill. Signature's at the bottom. J. Blair. Looks okay. He knows Blair. Still, he should check. He looks at the truck, Air Canada all right, at the two guys, faces in shadow under the parka hoods. They seem to know what they're doing. Doesn't want to look like a fool. Not in front of Shrimpton. Chuck reaches into his breast pocket, feels around, pats his jacket pockets.

"Hell," he says. "Don't have a pen. Have to go to the office."

"Here." Rick whips a ballpoint out of his parka pocket. He holds it out to Waters.

Waters hold the waybill against the side of the plane. He scribbles with the pen. Rick watches John and Shrimpton methodically loading boxes into the truck. Must be six now, seven. Waters shakes the pen.

"Damn!" he says. "Cold ink. Won't write. Come on, let's go inside."

Rick glances over at Berry. John has Ken's gun in his parka pocket. Is it time for the emergency plan? If Waters balks, they'll invite him along to check things out. Once he's in the truck they'll tie him up.

"Lets load 'er up first," John grunts, "then we'll . . . ."

Thunk. The conveyor belt stops. Box number nine is on its way down.

"Oh, hell!" says Shrimpton.

"Maybe she blew a fuse." Rick peers under the metal rollers as if he knew something about conveyor belts.

"Bloody thing never works!" says Shrimpton, banging on it with his fist.

"Cheap outfit you guys work for," laughs John.

"Damn right!" says Shrimpton.

"Come on, you guys," says Waters. "I'm freezin' my balls off out here."

Whirr. Thunkathunka. The conveyor belt starts up again as mysteriously as it had stopped. Waters is shivering now in his light jacket. He scribbles again with the pen. A blue streak. Ink! He signs his name at the bottom. Rick scribbles "Fred Davis" on the Transair waybills.

"Okay," he calls to John. "Let's go!"

He slams the back doors and they hop into the cab.

"Thanks for your help," John calls to Shrimpton as they drive off. "See ya 'round."

John and Rick drive back down the tarmac the way they'd come, straight towards the Air Canada freight office. It's 10:20 p.m.

Harold Goring is warming up in the shelter of the Esso refuelling station near the old hangar when he sees the white truck coming back. He's looked everywhere for those damn *Toronto Telegrams*. Not hide nor hair.

"Sure is in a hurry," he mutters as the truck comes speeding towards the Esso station, turns sharply and heads down the road out of the airport. Goring shuffles back to the terminal to report the disappearance of the *Toronto Telegrams*.

10:25 p.m. Ken looks at the luminous dial on his watch. It'll be done now. He sits still in the dark warehouse, ears cocked for cars, sirens, sounds of trouble. All quiet. Ten-thirty. Where the hell are they? He rubs his fist on the window making a hole in the frost and peers out. Five minutes late now. Trouble? He'd been a fool to hire amateurs. . . . Ken turns on the radio. CJOB. Always first with the news. That reporter, John Harvard, he'd have it. Sharp cookie. Ken paces the office humming along with the music. No news is good news.

The white stationwagon is still parked beside the Transair building and the light is still shining through the window when John wheels the Air Canada truck into the parking lot and backs it up to his convertible.

"Let's make it quick," he whispers, opening the trunk.

Rick grabs a box from the back of the truck.

"Holy Mary!" Rick stumbles as he lugs the box towards the car. The box slips out of his hands, slides down his leg and lands on his foot. Rick groans, clutches his ankle, doubles up in pain.

"For Chrissakes, you'll wake up the whole goddamn city!" John whispers at him hoarsely.

"God, I think it's broken!" Rick writhes on the dirty snow, glove stuffed in his mouth to keep from crying out.

John works feverishly transferring the boxes from the trunk to the car trunk. For two cents he'd put a bullet through that little cocksucker's head. Of all the dumb . . . ! His arms feel like jelly.

"Look out." he says. "I'm going to back in closer." He jumps into the convertible, starts the engine and backs towards the truck, leaning out the driver's door.

Crunch. The open door has caught a fence post sticking out of a snowdrift.

"Fuck!" John pulls the door closed. The armrest comes off in his hand. The door is smashed in.

Rick limps over and sits on the tail of the truck. He drags boxes to the edge and dumps them into the car's trunk. Tenforty. They strip off their parkas and coveralls and stuff them in on top.

10:45 p.m. Ken stops pacing to listen to the deejay's patter. Usual crap. What the hell is happening? Should've done it himself. What if they've split with the load?

Like a grey ghost the white convertible wheels into the lot beside Ken's stationwagon. Ken's out the door like a shot.

"Clean as a whistle," John pants. "But if you think I'm liftin' another ounce of that crap you can go screw yourself."

"Okay," says Ken. "Okay."

He counts the boxes. Metal straps unbroken. Twelve.

"I'll take it from here. Call me in the morning. Eight o'clock. Sharp. I'll have the rest of your dough."

Ken lifts the twelve boxes into the back of his stationwagon. Must be half a ton. Good thing he'd been brought up throwing sides of beef around.

As Ken's stationwagon pulls away from the warehouse, its tail end almost dragging on the ground, Fred McKay turns out the light in his office in the Transair building, locks up and starts the engine in his white stationwagon. Funny, there's an Air Canada truck parked in the back of the lot, lights off, at an odd angle, almost blocking the entrance. What's it doing there? Breakdown probably. Froze up. Caretaker'll deal with it in the morning.

Ken drives carefully through the city, radio on. No news. No cops. No traffic. He can't believe it. Almost an hour since the gold has disappeared and nothing is happening! Maybe he should head straight for the country. . . . No, play it safe. Stick to plan.

He drives east on Ellice, past Harry's hangout, the Happy Vineyard, turns south on Broadway, across the Osborne Street bridge, south on Osborne and left on Balfour. He stops at the end, number 119, a small, square bungalow a lot like his old house on Lindsay Street.

"Real sorry to bother you so late," Ken apologizes to the grey-haired woman in pin curls who opens the door. "Harry said I could use his freezer. Got a load of moose-meat here. Don't want it to spoil. Only take a minute."

"Well, okay," says Harry Backlin's mother-in-law.

Once more Ken carries the gold bricks, one by one, through Harry's back door and down the basement. He stacks eleven of them neatly in Harry's freezer and covers them with packages of frozen vegetables and pies. Jeez, he forgot to ask Harry for the key! No matter. He'll be back in the morning. He shuts the lid.

The twelfth and last box Ken stuffs into an old leather briefcase he finds in Harry's den. He pushes up a tile in the artificial rec room ceiling, heaves the briefcase up on to a rafter and replaces the tile. Nobody'll think to look there, not even Harry.

Ken flicks off the lights and climbs back into his car. Eleven forty-five. Gotta get home. Elva'll think he's screwing some chick! Ha, ha!

Ken pulls away too excited to notice the dark figure that emerges from the shadow of Harry's garage or the car that guns away from the next block a moment later, a white Ford convertible with a smashed door and no tail-lights.

The French Connection

MARCH 1, 1966; 11:50 P.M.

Chuck Waters is tidying the papers on his desk. Forty minutes to quitting time. He's counting every one. The airport is silent as a tomb. The shrill of the telephone makes him jump.

"Waters?"

"Yeah?"

"Pete Leveille. Air Canada cargo. Where's your shipment?"

A feather of fear tickles the back of Waters' neck.

"What shipment?"

"You know, Red Lake. We were called at 7:30 p.m. to expect twelve bars of gold bullion at 10 p.m. tonight. We're still waitin'."

"You picked it up."

"Like hell we did!"

"I got the waybills right here. Signed, sealed, delivered. Two of your guys in a truck."

Sergeant Hank Hanis of the St. James police force takes the phone call from Pete Leveille just before midnight. Half a million dollars in gold bullion has vanished into thin air. A squad car is at the Winnipeg airport within four minutes. The trail is stone cold. Hanis calls his chief, George Maltby. Maltby's sound asleep in bed. He tells Hanis to call out the detectives and goes back to sleep. He'll need his rest. It's going to be a hard week.

March 2; 1 a.m.

Rick Grenkow is stretched out on a couch, nursing his throbbing, bruised foot in cold towels. He has his arm around Sandra Ans, a cute kid, secretary at the Compact vacuum cleaner company. Rick's always given Sandra the eye, for business reasons more than anything. Always good to be in with head office. He'd seen a light in her apartment window driving home down Maryland Street that night.

"It's Rick," he said, tapping on her door. "Come on, I'll buy ya a drink."

Sandra didn't want to let him in. Her hair was up in curlers and she looked a mess. Rick was persistent.

"Gimme a coffee then."

"What's the matter?" she said as he limped into the room. Rick was dressed to kill, as usual, but he looked rumpled, tired and there was a big rip in his pant leg.

"Testing a machine," Rick grinned. "Dropped the damn thing on my foot. Some housewife I'd make, eh?"

They watch the late movie grind to a tearful end. Rick jumps when the news flash comes on. It gives him a boost like a shot of straight hooch. Wow. Sounds pretty impressive on TV. He leafs through the phone book. Aqua-Terra Motel, 1792 Pembina Highway.

"Hear it?" he asks John Berry.

"Yeah. You okay?"

"Sure."

John senses something in Rick's voice, a small quaver of uncertainty. What if he panics? Runs? Goes to the hospital?

"Come on over," he says. "I got company. She'll find a friend. We'll have a little party."

Joe Krier, owner and manager of the Aqua-Terra Motel, is closing up when Rick gets there. John Berry had got him out of bed, checking in at midnight. Joe didn't mind that much. Berry was a regular customer, free with his booze, his dough. Business was slow in the winter. Krier liked to hang around, doing little extras, making John feel at home. He felt a little sorry for these guys, on the road all the time.

"What time do you open up in the morning Joe?" Rick asks, nodding at the switchboard.

"Nine."

"Jeez," says Rick, wrinkling his forehead. "Got a call to make. Real big deal. Eight sharp."

"No problem," says Krier. "Glad to help."

The sky is barely grey when Joe Krier slams off the alarm, struggles out of bed and opens the office at 8 a.m. Right away the line from unit one lights up. Must be pretty important to get Grenkow out of bed at this time of day.

"Get me 339-7804, will ya Joe?"

Krier writes the number on a little pad he keeps by the switchboard. He tries to keep a record of all calls so he doesn't get stung for long distance, besides the cops sometimes nose around. Can't be too careful these days, all these crooks running around, Mafia, the guy on the eight o'clock news was saying. Who else could've pulled a heist as slick as that? Joe's mind is running on the gold robbery as he puts the call through. One ring.

"Hello." A man's voice. Deep.

"Good morning."

"How are you this morning?"

"Okay."

Joe Krier keeps listening. He's not in the habit of eavesdropping on his customers' phone calls but there's something in the tone of Rick's voice, a mystery, an urgency, that keeps him hooked.

"Your birthday cake is ready. You set to roll?"

"Damn right."

"Okay. You meet your contact at Brandon and follow the sun. Got any money?"

"No."

"Meet me at the Bay. Paddlewheel restaurant. Ten o'clock. It would be best if you're not seen with John. . . ."

Krier hears a noise at the door. He quickly switches off the call.

Sharp at 9:30 a.m. Ken turns up at the parole office, grinning, hand outstretched.

"Hiya!" he beams at his "conscience," John Veccione. "Bet you're surprised to see me this morning! Everybody on the radio's saying it's a Leishman job. The Flying Bandit strikes again! Well here I am! Pure as the driven snow."

Veccione smiles with relief. The same thoughts had, in fact, crossed his mind.

"Glad to see you, Ken."

"Mind if I run down to Treherne for a day? My granddad's not feeling too good. Might not last long. Been a real father to me."

"Sure. Don't see why not."

When the police call a few minutes later Veccione tells them Ken Leishman is safe and well in Winnipeg.

At 10 a.m. Rick Grenkow spots Ken's bald head at the back of the Paddlewheel as he gets off the escalator. Rick's excited, proud, jumpy, not yet used to walking through crowds of shoppers without sensing a heavy hand on his shoulder. When he overhears snatches of conversation about the robbery, *his* robbery, he wants to poke people and shout, Hey! I'm the guy! I did it! Aren't you surprised?

"Nice work," says Ken. "Beautiful." He shoves an envelope across to Rick. Rick opens it. Five hundred dollar bills.

"Hey!" Rick says. "Where the fuck's the rest? Where's John's share?"

"You'll get it. When Harry's back."

"Oh sure! We'll be in Vancouver!"

"You'll get it. And a lot more. Later. It's the best I can do for now. I'm being watched."

10:15 a.m. A white Ford convertible pulls up in front of 119 Balfour Avenue.

"Hi," says the good-looking young man. "Friend of Harry's. Come to pick up a parcel. Delivered last night."

"Do you mean the moose-meat?"

"Huh?"

"Well," says Harry's mother-in-law tartly, "the only thing that was delivered last night was a load of moose-meat. It must have been a very large moose."

John Berry laughs out loud. That Ken! What a card!

He finds the freezer right away, shoves aside the pies and frozen peas, wraps one box of gold in an old pink bedspread he'd found in the trunk and walks back out to his car with the parcel tucked under his arm.

Ken, he says to himself, you're a smart cookie, but you're not as smart as you think you are.

Berry drives west through River Heights then out Portage Avenue. He's past the city limits, nearing Headingley, when he sees the flashing lights of a police roadblock. Oh, no. At Nick's Cafe Berry skids the convertible on to a gravel road and heads south towards the Assiniboine River. He hides the box of gold under some brush in a secluded spot on the riverbank, then, his load lightened, whistling to himself, he turns back to the highway and heads west.

Winnipeg is in a paroxysm of pleasure. A city fond of rebels and underdogs, irreverent, suspicious of authority, familiar with theft on many levels, Winnipeg loves a good story and even more it loves a joke. The gold caper, sweet as a chinook at the end of a cold, dark winter, is a beaut. Not only has Goldfinger struck right under its very nose but the police, the airlines, the gold mines and the Royal Canadian Mint have been made to look like idiots. Hooray! Nothing this exciting has happened in Winnipeg since the Great Flood of 1950. Work grinds to a halt as everywhere, on streetcorners, in buses, in pubs and offices and kitchens, people stop to gabble about the gold robbery, and everywhere the same secret wish is whispered: "Gee, I hope they get away with it!"

The police don't think it's funny. Three police forces are working on the gold robbery: the small St. James police department, in charge of the municipality in which the airport is located; the RCMP, in charge of security at the airport, and the Winnipeg police who probably have the best idea of who might have done it. As well, the FBI, Scotland Yard and Interpol have been alerted. Among them the police haven't a clue.

The exact value of the stolen gold is pegged at $383,497. A reward of ten percent of the total value is offered. Everyone in Winnipeg turns detective. All the paranoiac fantasies of a peaceful prairie population burst like a cloudburst over the open-line radio shows, the newspaper offices. The phones at police headquarters start ringing off the hook: a strange hearse had been spotted near the airport early in the morning; a conversation about gold had been overheard in a bar a week before; someone called Long John from Toronto was in town looking for gold, strange noises were heard, suspicious cars were seen. . . .

The police patiently check out each tip.

The airport area is cordoned off and turned inside out. Every employee is grilled. On Ellice Avenue a motorist searching in his trunk for tools to fix a flat is startled to find himself suddenly surrounded by cruiser cars. A Red Lake passenger on flight 108 is searched and questioned before being allowed to go on to Chicago.

Chuck Waters desperately racks his brain trying to remember. What did they look like? Tall? Short? Fat? Glasses? Gloves? How did they talk? Accent? Dark? Fair? What did they say? He answers the same questions over and over and over.

"I dunno," he sighs, rubbing his eyes. "Ordinary guys. Couldn't see their faces. I had my eyes on the gold all the time." He's sick with worry, exhaustion, humiliation. Christ, he's got to be the biggest asshole in Canada. Get the sack for sure. If they don't throw him in jail. Shrimpton is more philosophical. "Better than a gun in the gut, Chuck. We could have been two cold pieces of meat." Neither Shrimpton nor John Workman, who'd been up in the hold pushing gold bars down the conveyor belt, can offer any description of the thieves.

The Air Canada truck is found where it had been left in the Transair parking lot. It is searched and dusted for fingerprints. Nothing. There are footprints and tire tracks in the snow but since the area is heavily travelled they don't amount to much. An RCMP constable notices that a fence post has a fresh gash in it. He picks some fragments of orange plastic out of the wood and files them away.

2 p.m. Ken calls Harry Backlin in Los Angeles. Harry hasn't gone to Mexico after all, like he'd told his friends. He'd caught the flu in Vancouver and stayed on for a while, then gone on to San Francisco and Los Angeles, mixing a little business with pleasure.

"Hiya, Harry!" says Ken. "Having a good time?"

"Great. How about you?"

"Terrific! Listen, a couple of friends have got a present for you. A whole moose! Must have weighed a ton. I cut it up and put it in your freezer."

"Jesus Christ!"

"It's okay, Harry. Safe as a church."

"You fucking crazy bastard!"

Ken holds the receiver away from his ear to blunt the force of Harry's shouts and curses. Jeez, Ken says to himself, you pull the slickest robbery in Canadian history and that's all the thanks you get!

"Relax, Harry," he says at last. "I'll move the stuff out tomorrow. I hope you've got some, uh, friends who'll take it."

Ken cheers up when he reads the newspaper accounts of the heist. Front page. Big headlines. Lots of pictures. He carefully cuts them out and pastes them in his scrapbook.

March 3, 1966: 3:40 p.m.

John Berry and Rick Grenkow are stopped by an RCMP roadblock just east of Swift Current, Saskatchewan. Their two cars have been clocked by a highway patrol at speeds of 100 miles per hour. The officer checks their driver's licences and directs them to the magistrate at Swift Current to pay their fines.

Ken calls the butcher who's taken over from Tommy Reece at Treherne. Sure, he has lots of space in his meat locker. Ken's welcome, any time. Fine, says Ken, I'll bring the moose-meat out tonight. Just leave the key out for me.

"Take it easy," says the butcher. "It's blowin' to beat hell out here. Real white-out. Blizzard warning."

The cutting edge of the blizzard is already whistling into Winnipeg from the west, whisking puffs of snow into white whirlpools. Bad night. Ken is uneasy. He's got to unload the gold, but what if he gets stuck in a snowdrift? Goes off the highway? It's a hundred miles to Treherne. Stationwagon'll be heavy. Cops'll be out. Bad luck.

Ken shows up at Harry's door after supper with gunny sacks. Harry's mother-in-law is glad to see the end of the meat. She knows that lawyers have a lot of strange clients, some of them criminals, and that clients often pay in strange ways, especially if they're buddies, and Harry has a lot of buddies, drinking buddies, hunting buddies, but Harry always went hunting in the autumn. Harry's mother-in-law believes that mothers-in-law should mind their own business, but she's been around long enough to know that a dead moose in March is probably a hot moose so she isn't too surprised when Ken bounds up the basement stairs pale as a ghost.

"Yes," she says. "Yesterday morning. Nice young man. Fair, blue eyes. Very polite. Here only a minute. Lovely car. From Alberta."

Ken closes his eyes. When he gets his hands on that double-crossing. . . .

"Is anything wrong?"

"No," Ken smiles. "Friend of mine."

In the basement, Ken reaches up into the ceiling and pulls down the briefcase. He grabs a screwdriver and pries open the box of gold. The ingot nestles in its padding, gleaming yellow, soft and smooth as butter. Wow! Beautiful! Ken runs his fingertips lightly over the surface. He can hardly resist taking it home. Show Elva. Maybe he should take them all home, hide them in the basement, in the cosmetic boxes. Heck, he's got to do something. Harry's coming home tomorrow. What if Berry shows up again? Maybe Berry's gone to the cops, set a trap. What if Berry tries to unload the bar, gets caught? Ken listens to the wind howl outside. He watches the snow pile up outside the basement window. It gives him an idea. The perfect hiding place!

March 4, 1966.

The Great Blizzard hits Winnipeg with winds of near hurricane force. Visibility is zero, snow is driven into ten-foot drifts. Cars are buried; buses grind to a halt, beached in snowdrifts like giant whales. Streets are blocked; schools and offices close. Thousands of shoppers and workers are trapped in stores and factories miles from home. Emergency forces get around on skis and ski-doos, babies are delivered at home and in stalled taxis; the sick are pulled to hospital on toboggans. Total strangers bunk down together in Eaton's furniture department, in clubs and restaurants and hotels; blankets and pillows are rustled up out of peculiar places and bottles of booze mysteriously appear from nowhere. Most people are so high on the adventure they don't need a drink. After the first panic passes, the anxiety of frustration and helplessness, people relax. They settle in to enjoy the storm, awestruck, overwhelmed, snug as bugs in a rug. Everyone has a wonderful time. Nothing this exciting has hit Winnipeg since, well, since the Great Gold Robbery three days ago. It seems like a long time.

By Saturday, March 5, when Winnipeg is digging out of the snow, the first hints of a new thrill come in from the east, a tacky sex scandal involving a former cabinet minister Pierre Sevigny and a mysterious German prostitute named Gerda Munsinger. News of the gold robbery drops out of the Winnipeg press. The police have nothing to report anyway. The trail is cold.

Saturday, March 5; 7 p.m.
Ken strides casually through the Winnipeg airport carrying an old leather briefcase. Harry's plane's due in any minute. Ken waits for him by the CP Air baggage carousel. To pass the time he counts cops. One, by the door, two, by the escalator, three, by the gate, all standing very erect and mumbling importantly into their walkie-talkies.

"Hiya, Harry!" Ken waves.

"Hi," says Harry, glancing around. "Christ, you son-of-a-bitch," he hisses between his teeth. "What the hell are you doin' here?"

"Car's snowed in," says Ken cheerfully. "I'll drive you home."

"What's in the bag?" asks Harry in the car.

"It's a surprise, Harry," grins Ken. "Wait'll you see it. It'll knock your eyes out!"

Harry knows that briefcase. It's his.

Monday, March 7, 1966.
The fresh snow is sparkling in the warm sunlight. The sudden thaw has surprised everyone. The snow is simply melting away.

Ken listens to the water running down the eavestrough outside his basement office window. He tests the door on his office. Locked. Good. He heaves Harry's briefcase up on his desk. His hand is shaking. He's got to move fast.

He'll go to Hong Kong, Tokyo maybe, if that doesn't work out. The Orient has a big appetite for gold. It can be sold for two, three times its value on the black market. All Ken needs is a tiny scrap, just a sample. Once he makes contact a courier'll pick up the rest of the shipment. Easy as pie. Ken had thought he'd try the States first, maybe Chicago, but the Winnipeg *Tribune* had run a story a couple of days back speculating that Hong Kong would be the smart place for a thief to unload the stolen gold bullion. Ken thought it was pretty dumb of the authorities to be giving free advice but then it matched their conduct in the rest of the case. The *Free Press* had also been helpful. It quoted geologist Dr. G.M. Brownell as saying that the thief "could easily reduce the bars to a more manageable size by cutting them in pieces with a hacksaw."

Ken pulls a hacksaw out of his toolbox. He reaches into the old leather briefcase and pulls out a moneybelt, then the gold brick in its shattered wooden box. He places them all on his desk.

Ken stares at the gold brick. It looks funny sitting there on his desk blotter among his papers. Some paperweight! It has a nice glow. Ken still gets a kick out of looking at it. He can hardly believe he's really pulled it off.

Ken places the bar of gold gingerly on the edge of his desk and starts sawing off a piece about one inch long. A thin spray of gold dust drifts to the floor as a line appears in the bar. Shit! He's wasting a fortune! He carefully places a sheet of newspaper under the bar.

Jeez, it takes forever to saw through that gold! Beads of sweat are standing out on his forehead. His arm aches. When he's finished he lifts the mutilated bar back into its box and puts it in the briefcase. He carefully pours the gold dust into an empty pill bottle and stows it at the back of his workbench among the nails. Then he tucks the small piece of gold into the moneybelt and straps it around his waist next to his skin. He's never heard of anyone getting a body search going out of the country. It's what you bring in that counts. Coming back he'll be clean as a whistle.

It's afternoon when Ken saunters into Harry's office in the Power Building, briefcase in hand.

"Hiya, Harry," he says. "Going to Hong Kong. Can you let me have a loan?"

Ken had tried to talk Harry into going to Hong Kong. Safe as a church. Sorry, said Harry. His passport hadn't come through. Harry had overlooked one thing in his application: he had been born Harry Backewich. He'd changed his name. Whoever heard of a lawyer called Backewich? That was no sweat, half the hunkies in Winnipeg passed as WASPs, but Harry had neglected to enclose a change of name certificate with his passport application. His passport was delayed. Ken's kind of relieved. The waiting around is driving him nuts. He feels better having things in his own hands. He'll have it all fixed up by the weekend, be back home Sunday night. Trouble is he's broke. The return fare to Hong Kong is $973. He'll need another $500 at least for living expenses. Can't look like a bum.

"How much?" says Harry.

"Couple of grand."

"Who do ya think I am? Rockefeller?"

"Look," says Ken, desperate. "I'm strapped, Harry."

Although Harry Backlin has known Ken for eight years, acted for him, shot the shit with him countless times, listened to his plans, encouraged, Harry has not been perfectly frank.

Harry is broke. It's not the kind of secret a guy confesses easily even to his best friend. Ken admires Harry, respects him, envies him. Harry enjoys it, he has to admit. He likes to show off for Ken, playing Mr. Moneybags, hot shot lawyer, picking up the tab, drinking Chivas Regal, bragging about the deals he was making, five grand here, ten there. Bullshit. Sure, Harry makes money, but he spends it too, dumping dough into hare-brained schemes that go sour, gambling and losing, always digging himself out of the hole. When it comes to managing money Harry's almost as bad as Ken.

"I'll see what I can do," says Harry.

Harry reserves a seat on CP Air flight 401 leaving Vancouver for Hong Kong at 4 p.m. March 9. He makes the reservation in his own name and puts it on his American Express card. He also books a roomette in his own name on the CPR Canadian leaving Winnipeg that night at 10:45 p.m., due into Vancouver at noon on Wednesday, March 9. Harry makes an appointment with a friend of his, Dr. W.G. French, for Ken to get a smallpox vaccination. He promises to wire Ken some money to the Vancouver airport.

"Gee," says Ken. "Thanks. You're a pal, Harry. Mind if I leave the briefcase here? I'll pick it up when I get back."

"Make it fast," Harry snaps.

Ken is in Dr. French's office that afternoon at three o'clock. Dr. French recognizes him right away: he's the man who met Harry Backlin at the airport Saturday night. Dr. French had been in Vancouver the night of the gold robbery; he'd flown back to Winnipeg on March 5 on the same flight as Harry. The name Ken Leishman sounds familiar too. He can't quite place it.

Ken is vague about his travel plans. He might go to Hong Kong at Easter. He might go next week. Maybe tomorrow if his business deal heats up. Would the doctor mind backdating the vaccination certificate, just in case?

A smallpox vaccination requires a seven-day waiting period. Dr. French hesitates. He dates the certificate March 1, 1966.

At 9:45 p.m., Monday, March 7, Ken Leishman climbs aboard the CPR's Canadian, car 107, roomette 3, bound for Vancouver, with a six-pound piece of solid gold strapped around his waist.

Harry Backlin's reservations have not gone unnoticed. Police have alerted all airlines, railways, bus depots and travel agents to keep an eye out for suspicious people travelling to Vancouver, San Francisco and the Far East. It's a routine procedure. They don't have much hope. The police are almost certain the gold has long since left the country.

The name "Harry Backlin" sticks in the police dragnet like a tiny speck of dust. It's a not unfamiliar name to the Winnipeg police. There was the matter of some stolen mink pelts a few years back. Backlin's name had surfaced in the investigation but nothing could be proved against him. Backlin had some interesting clients too, men known to the police, men like Ken Leishman, with whom Harry seems to be on more than professional terms. Harry is worth watching. Harry is watched. His car is followed. His house is staked out.

Tuesday, March 8, 1966.

Dr. French is worried. It was a small fib, really, lying about the date, but. . . . Perhaps it was the date that triggered it, March 1, the date of the gold robbery, but he remembers now something in the press about Hong Kong, something to do with gold, and there's something troubling about the name Leishman, something unsavoury. He's probably just being silly. . . .

Dr. French broods until his anxiety is overwhelming. He's made a terrible mistake. It could look as if he were part of a conspiracy. Yet, to alert the police is to expose his own guilt. . . . It's only a hunch . . . probably nothing.

After work, over a stiff scotch in a quiet bar, Dr. French confides in one of his closest friends, Sergeant McCall of the St. Boniface police. It's only a tip, but. . . . McCall agrees to pass it on to the St. James police.

It's the hottest lead the police have had. Ken had been one of their prime suspects. The gold theft had his signature stamped all over it. They searched his car. Questioned him. Nothing.

"Not this time! Ha, ha!" Ken had mocked.

On Wednesday morning, March 9, John Veccione is questioned. Does Ken have permission to go to Hong Kong?

"Hong Kong?" gasps Veccione. "No!"

He calls Ken's house. Ken's out, says Elva. She's not sure where. Tell him to report in as soon as possible, says Veccione. He hasn't seen Ken for a week.

At 1 p.m. Harry Backlin dashes in to the CP Air ticket office at Portage and Main. Can't make his flight to Hong Kong this afternoon, he says. One of his boys is going instead. Can he change the reservation?

"Sure," says agent Louis Sylvestre. "What's the passenger's name?"

"Leishman. Ken Leishman."

"Address?"

"He'll pick it up."

Harry pays for the ticket by cheque. He wires Ken $500. It was all he could raise in two days.

As Harry walks out Sylvestre reaches for the telephone.

Ken walks into the Vancouver airport just after noon Vancouver time, two o'clock Winnipeg time. Four hours to kill before flight time. He calls Elva. She's frantic. His parole officer wants to see him. Now! What will she say?

"I'll be home tonight," says Ken. "Put him off."

Shit! What's happening? Who's squealed? Harry? What do they know? Ken's mind races as he heads for the CP Air ticket counter. He's in luck. A delayed flight is leaving for Winnipeg at 4 p.m. He buys a ticket.

"Leishman?" says the clerk, scratching his head. "I have a Leishman going to Hong Kong at 4 p.m. Are you the same man?"

"Yes."

The clerk hands him Harry's wire for $500.

"I have a message also, sir," he says, looking down, awkwardly, at his papers. "The RCMP would like you to drop by their office at your convenience, if you don't mind. It's right over there."

Ken follows the clerk's pointing finger with his eyes. The RCMP office is on the opposite side of the terminal through a set of glass doors.

"Fine," Ken grins, picking up his coat. He checks his suitcase through to Winnipeg and cancels his Hong Kong flight. He saunters leisurely in the direction of the RCMP office, sweating under his money belt. What's up? What will he do? Run for it? Where? No, he'd tried that before. Bluff it out. Play it cool.

Just before he reaches the office Ken turns down a corridor and doubles back to the airport gift shop. He buys some brown wrapping paper and a roll of string. In the privacy of a cubicle in the men's washroom he wraps the chunk of gold in the brown paper, ties it neatly and prints the address clearly on both sides:

Mr. H. Backlin,
303 Power Building,
Winnipeg,
Manitoba.

Ken throws the moneybelt in the garbage and takes his little parcel downstairs to the CP Air cargo department.

"Six pounds,' the agent says. "That's $3.80."

He fills out a waybill.

"Sender's name?"

"Pardon?"

"I need your name too."

"Leishman, Ken Leishman."

Ken saunters over to the RCMP office.

"Hiya," he says, sticking out his hand at the young corporal behind the desk. "Looking for me?"

The RCMP corporal is flustered.

"We've been asked to detain you, sir," he says apologetically, "but I have no further information. Orders haven't come through from Winnipeg yet."

"No problem," beams Ken. He helps himself to a chair, leans back, crosses his legs. "I'm in no hurry."

He was on his way to Tokyo, he says, to investigate some new Japanese aircraft he and a partner are planning to import to Canada. He's cancelled his trip. Must be some misunderstanding. Sure, he has permission to travel. Here's his passport, vaccination certificate, everything in order.

Ken is polite, friendly, eager to cooperate. He waits more than half an hour, chattering easily about flying, the aircraft business he and his partner, Harry Backlin, are setting up. The corporal is more and more embarrassed. This guy seems like a big shot. The RCMP has no reason to detain him. What if he makes trouble?

"Mind if I get a coffee?" Ken says, glancing at his watch. Two-thirty. "Care to join me?"

The corporal shakes his head. He walks Ken over to the coffee shop, watches him take a seat, order his coffee.

Ken sips it slowly, watching the cop out of the corner of his eye. Good! He's going! Ken finishes the cup, slips a quarter under the saucer and leaves. He walks rapidly downstairs to the CP Air cargo counter.

"Would it be too much trouble to return the parcel I left with you?" he asks the agent. "The man I sent it to has just arrived in Vancouver by plane."

"Sure," shrugs the agent. He hands Ken the little parcel and refunds his $3.80.

"Gee, thanks!" Ken beams.

"S'okay," says the agent.

Ken walks out of the terminal building with the package in his pocket. Half an hour later he comes back. His pocket is empty.

He boards CP Air flight 73 to Winnipeg at 3:45 p.m. He feels light-headed, elated. They can't hang anything on him, the suckers! He's clean as a whistle.

At four o'clock, just before take-off, Ken is taken off the plane by two RCMP officers. He is being held for questioning on parole violation. He is taken to the Richmond detachment, stripped and searched. His suitcase is searched. His trousers, tie, watch and shoelaces are taken away. Not an ounce of gold is found on him.

"Where's the package?" demands the RCMP corporal, waving the waybill. "Isn't that your signature?"

"I'm not answering any questions until I see my lawyer," says Ken, full of righteous indignation. "You have no right to hold me here. You haven't got a thing on me. You're barking up the wrong tree, I can tell you. You'd better watch it."

All he knows about the gold robbery, Ken says, is what he read in the newspapers.

Ken is locked up. In Winnipeg his house is turned inside out, even the cosmetics dumped out of their kits, his car taken apart. Harry Backlin's house is searched, even the freezer. Nothing.

The trail's so hot now the police can smell the gold.

Where is it?

Thursday, March 10, 1966; 11:30 a.m.

Five detectives arrive at Harry Backlin's office with a search warrant.

"Sure," says Harry. "Okay. Look, I've got a couple of clients. Give me a minute to deal with them, okay?"

Harry goes back into his inner office. The detectives nose around the waiting room, opening filing cabinets, turning up the cushions on the couches.

Winnipeg detective George Birnie spots an old leather briefcase behind the coat rack. He lifts it on to a chair. Whew, it's heavy. Birnie flips it open and looks inside. Beneath some maps and file folders he sees a splintered wooden box with a red seal and "Madsen Red Lake Gold Mines" stencilled on it. Inside it is the remains of a gold bar, serial number MRL 3330.

"I've got it!" cries Birnie.

He carries the briefcase into Harry's office.

"Do you know what's in this briefcase, Harry?"

"Yeah," says Harry. "Gold."

"Is this briefcase yours?"

"Nope. Belongs to a client. He left it here."

"What's his name?"

"I can't tell you."

"Do you know that you may be charged with illegal possession of gold bullion?"

"Yeah, yeah."

"I have to warn you, Harry, that anything you say. . . ."

"Sure, sure," says Harry. "I know I'm in trouble. Possession of stolen goods. But it's not my fault. I can explain."

"We'll have to take you in."

Harry Backlin is bundled off to the Winnipeg police station in the company of Winnipeg's largest, toughest detective, Peter van der Graff. But Harry isn't going to run. He's going to talk himself out of this one.

"Bet you're surprised, eh?" he asks van der Graff.

"You can say that again."

"I'm not worried," says Harry. "I got a good explanation. Look, my hands are steady. Guess I'll need a good lawyer, eh? Ha, ha!"

In the interrogation room Harry gives a brief formal statement:

"I know absolutely nothing about the theft of gold and, although I have been found in possession of gold bullion, it was left in my office without my knowledge, consent, request or authorization. I have a good idea of a number of people who could have left it there, and, as a matter of fact, on my own I was attempting in the last two days to discover the party or parties responsible. Had I another two or three days I could have located the person or persons who placed me in this position. It is my intention to cooperate with the authorities in their investigation of this matter."

"Is there anything else you can tell us, Harry?" asks van der Graff.

"Nope. That's it." Harry signs the statement.

He is left alone in the interrogation room. He smokes. He thinks. One hour passes. Two. At 2:30 p.m. detective John Main comes in to the outer office. Harry knows him. Good head.

"Hey, John!" he calls. "Come 'ere."

Main goes over.

"What's all this nonsense, you guys searching the houses of friends of mine?" says Harry. "It's embarrassing. To them and to me. You won't find the gold where you're lookin'."

"Yeah?" Main motions to detective Jack Taylor to come in. "Shut the door, you guys."

"Well, where is it, Harry?" asks Main.

"I don't know," says Harry. "But I might be able to help you. It depends on what you can do for me."

"Not a thing, Harry."

"Have you been to my house?"

"Yeah."

"Try the garage?"

"Yeah."

"Try around the garage?"

"Hell, Harry, the snow's six feet deep out there!"

Harry rubs his forehead.

"You think we might find some gold in your yard, is that right?" asks Main.

"Yeah, it's possible. If I were you fellows I'd look around the garage, between the garage and the yard next door. You might find some gold under the snow."

"Hey!" calls Taylor, grabbing his parka, "We're goin' back to Balfour!"

Harry is left alone in the small room, chain smoking, watching the detectives through the open door. Watchin' his own funeral, he says to himself. Sergeant Birnie comes in at 3:30 p.m.

"Hey, Birnie!" calls Harry, beckoning him over. "If I co-operate in finding the gold, what's in it for me?

"I can't do a thing," says Birnie. "I can ask the boss."

"Okay," says Harry. "I'll see him."

The boss, detective superintendent Norm Stewart, says Harry should speak to Chief Maltby. It's Maltby's case. As it happens he's just down the hall.

"I know I'm on the spot," Harry pleads to Maltby. "I know it looks bad. I'm not trying to hide anything. I knew it was there. I'm telling everything I know, believe me."

Maltby says nothing.

"Chief," Harry goes on. "I believe I can help you. I want to help you. But before I do, what are you prepared to do for me in return?"

"What do you mean, you can help?"

"I had nothing to do with the theft of the gold. But I have an idea who it might be. I can help you find out."

"Was it Leishman?"

"Leishman didn't have anything to do with it."

"Did you know Leishman had booked a flight to Hong Kong?"

"Nope."

"Have you any idea what business Leishman may have in Hong Kong?"

"He's into all kinds of deals. Could be in connection with his cosmetics business."

"Did you pay for his passage?"

"No, I did not."

Harry wipes his face with his handkerchief. His hands are shaking now.

"Look, chief. I want to cooperate but I need help. I have a wife and child. My mother-in-law is on the verge of a nervous breakdown over this. I think I can help you find the gold. What can you do for me in return?"

Maltby says nothing.

Harry clears his throat. Swallows.

"Surely you don't have to charge me if you find the gold?"

"You're a lawyer, Mr. Backlin," says Maltby. "You understand my position as chief of police. I can't be party to any deals. You will certainly be charged with possession of the bar of gold in your office."

Harry sobs.

"That will be the end of me! I've worked all my life for this!"

"I can't make any promises, Mr. Backlin. All I can do is submit my report."

"Okay," Harry sighs. "I'll show you where the gold is. But I don't want a crowd of Winnipeg policemen around my house."

"So it's at your house, then?"

"No, it's not in my house."

"Let's take a look."

In Vancouver Ken is interrogated all day by several RCMP officers including Scotty Gardiner, the corporal in charge of the investigation who has flown out from Winnipeg. Ken doesn't crack. He sticks to his Tokyo story. He's going to purchase aircraft. Start a pilot training school. Harry Backlin's his business partner. So what?

"Gold's been found," says Gardiner. "Backlin's office."

"Jeez!" cries Ken. "Who would have believed it, eh? And him a lawyer too!"

"Backlin's cooperating. He's made a statement. He's going to help us. Game's up, Ken."

Ken laughs. "Guess I'll have to get myself another lawyer!"

Thursday, March 10, 1966; 4 p.m.

Long lines of kids are streaming out of Riverview School at the end of Balfour Avenue. They spot the squad cars right away.

"Cops!" shouts David Korven, Backlin's paperboy. "It's a stakeout!"

Men in blue coats are standing on street corners, in lanes, in the schoolyard, on Harry Backlin's front steps. Cruiser cars block the street at both ends.

The kids head for Backlin's house like a swarm of bees. Nothing this exciting has happened in Riverview since, well, since the Great Blizzard last week.

A dozen cops are standing in Harry's backyard. Two are on their hands and knees, groping in the snow near the garage. A fat, red-faced Mountie is digging furiously into an eight-foot snowdrift. In their excitement the combined forces of the Winnipeg, St. James and Royal Canadian Mounted Police have forgotten to bring shovels. They share Harry's. Inspector

W.F.G. Perry of the RCMP, being scientific, probes the snow-drifts with a broomstick.

Harry is standing by the back door next to Chief Maltby.

"You might want to try over here," he says, waving towards a big drift about ten feet from the back door.

"I've got something!" Perry shouts, feeling a solid bump against the end of his stick.

The fat Mountie digs. He digs and digs and digs. About four feet down a wooden box is uncovered. Then another. And another. Four.

"If I were you, I'd try over here," says Harry, gesturing towards his wife's Volkswagen parked by the garage. Sweating, changing shifts, the cops move to another drift.

The huge crowd of kids and neighbours oohs and aahhs as the boxes are dug up. News photographers are standing on cars, roofs, snapping away and radio reporters stick their microphones in people's faces. Whose house? What's happening? How many boxes? Is it the gold?

Three boxes are found by the Volkswagen and three more near the back sidewalk. David Korven had shovelled it only the day before. He'd come within a foot of the gold.

Ten boxes. One more in Harry's office makes eleven. Where's the last? Harry shakes his head.

"I'd be very surprised if you found it here," he says. "In fact I'm surprised you found as many as you did."

Vancouver, March 10, 1966; 9 p.m.

Ken is seething. Harry, the fink! The weasel! The sleazy son-of-a-bitch! Taking them right to the gold, meek as a lamb! Just to save his own neck! All his work shot to hell.

Ken had almost fainted when the cops told him the gold had been found, but he stayed cool, collected. Never blinked an eye. Pretty stupid, was all he'd said. So what? It's none of his business. The cops couldn't pin a thing on him. They'd have to let him go.

He's back in his cage now, pacing back and forth, back and forth. There are two other prisoners, a drunk sleeping off his hangover and a punk kid doing ten days for dangerous driving. A new prisoner is shoved into the cage just after nine o'clock, ordinary guy, about Ken's age, dressed in casual clothes, brown chinos, windbreaker, Hush Puppies. Just another bum.

"Got a smoke?" he asks Ken.

Ken shakes his head.

"Shit." The stranger shrugs out of his windbreaker and sits on a bench across from Ken, head against the wall, eyes closed. Ken watches him. Something familiar about his style. Looks like a con. Might be a good guy to know. Ken sits up, alert, curious.

"What you in for?"

"Suspicion of burglary!" The stranger snorts, spits. "Found a crowbar and a pair of snips in my car. Christ, a guy can't carry a tool kit around without landing in the can! Assholes! Well, I got me a good lawyer. I'll be outa here in the morning, I can tell ya. How about you? Drunk driving?"

Ken flushes, angry.

"You hear about the big gold robbery in Winnipeg?"

"Yeah! sure! Hell, that was some job, eh! Whooee!"

"That was my baby."

"You're kiddin!" The stranger stares at Ken. Then he doubles over and slaps his knee.

"Haw, haw! Tell me another! That's rich!"

Ken is furious now.

"What's so damn funny?"

"That was a smart job, a real pro job. I heard some lawyer done it. Now you don't look like no lawyer to me, sucker. You don't dress like a lawyer. Lookit them shoes, crap, cheap crap. Naw. You know what you look like to me? Paperhanger. Bum cheques. Credit cards. Real two-bit stuff."

Ken speaks coolly and precisely.

"My name is Ken Leishman and I'm being held in connection with the theft of half a million dollars in gold from the Winnipeg airport. You can check it out yourself."

"Aw, come on! There were two guys took that stuff. Young guys."

"It was my idea. I engineered it. I figured it all out. I hired the two guys who pulled it off. I was on my way to Hong Kong to dispose of the gold when they picked me up."

"Nail you with the stuff?"

"Naw!" Ken laughs. "Gave me plenty of time to ditch it. I told them I threw it in the river by the airport. They have

half the police force out there right now combing the riverbank with dogs! That'll keep 'em busy!"

Ken explains the robbery patiently. The stranger listens
quietly, making little snorts of amazement and appreciation.
Ken can tell he's impressed. He's glad of a friendly ear, glad
of a chance to talk after all these weeks keeping everything
bottled up inside until he's ready to explode. Heck, it *was* a
great job, if only Harry. . . .

"What if he squeals, your lawyer buddy?"

Ken laughs bitterly.

"Good old Harry! He's got no guts. Probably spilling the
whole story to them right now. Sucking cock. Jeez, four
hundred lawyers in Winnipeg would've jumped at the deal
but I had to pick him! Stupid bastard!"

Ken's reserve crumbles before the torrent of his rage against
Harry. The stranger listens sympathetically, offering advice.
Ken begins to feel hopeful.

"I can beat it," he says, pounding his fist on the bench.
"It'll be his word against mine. Harry's word against mine.
I'll get a good lawyer. Jew lawyer. They're the best. Some
young kid who'll fight like a tiger for the publicity. I'll beat
it!"

By lights-out at 11 p.m. Ken and the stranger are on first
name terms. Ken and Al. Al Clark his name is, lives in Vancouver, done time. Nice guy, Ken figures, not too smart. Pes-
ters him with dumb questions. Like how was Ken going to
explain all this sudden money?

"Won it in Vegas!" Ken had laughed. "Who's to know?"
The more he thought about the robbery the better he liked
it. Wouldn't change a thing.

"Listen," Al whispers the next morning. "I'll be outa here
in an hour. Maybe I can help ya out, unload that little piece
of gold for ya. I got contacts, ya know what I mean. You'll
need dough. I can make a little profit."

Ken shakes his head. Heck, tell Al Clark where the gold
is and he'll never see him again! What kind of sucker does
Clark take him for?

"Thanks," Ken says politely. "They might be staking it out.
Get you into trouble. Thanks for the offer."

"Good luck, buddy," says Clark. "See ya around."

Friday, March 11, 1966, Ken is returned to Winnipeg in RCMP custody. He is kept in jail while the police check out the names and phone numbers found in Ken's address book.

On the morning of March 16, John Berry is arrested in his room at the Blue Boy Motel in Vancouver. Rick Grenkow is picked up at a girlfriend's house in Vancouver the same afternoon and Paul Grenkow is nabbed sitting in his car outside the office of the Compact vacuum cleaner agencies. All deny they know anything about the gold theft.

March 18, 1966, Ken Leishman, Harry Backlin, John Berry, Rick and Paul Grenkow are charged in Winnipeg magistrate's court with theft and conspiracy to steal $383,497 in gold bullion from the Winnipeg International Airport. None has confessed, not even Harry, who sticks to his story that eleven gold bars found their way into his possession by mysterious means.

May 2, 1966, the preliminary hearing opens in Winnipeg. The police have rounded up dozens of witnesses: Harold Goring, still complaining about the missing *Telegrams*; Joe Krier of the Aqua-Terra Motel, Sandra Ans, Rick's girlfriend; Steve Hyra, the beer waiter they got so chummy with at the Black Knight room; the cop who stopped Berry and Grenkow for speeding at Swift Current; Dr. W.G. French. . . . For more than two weeks the Crown laboriously builds its case: plane tickets, train reservations, Paul's motel receipts, Ken's calls to Harry in San Francisco, bits of wood and sealing wax in the trunk of Berry's car, pieces of plastic from the armrest which match the fragments found embedded in the fence post, Ken's phone number on Joe Krier's notepad. . . .

Ken sits behind his young Jewish lawyer, Mel Myers, listening intently. His spirits rise as the hearing progresses. The Crown's case is full of holes. No positive identification. No fingerprints. No confessions. Nothing but scraps. Coincidences. All circumstantial. Sure, they found some microscopic traces of gold dust in his pant cuffs. Ken can blow that to hell.

Ken is laughing, cracking jokes the morning of May 17, 1966, when the bottom falls out of his world. A familiar face is taking the stand. Ken hardly recognizes him with his fresh haircut, eyeglasses and neatly pressed dark blue suit. Al Clark places his hand on the Bible and swears that he is an undercover agent for the RCMP. His real name is Allan James Richards, a fifteen-year veteran with the RCMP. He was deliberately placed in Ken's cell to extract incriminating information. He succeeded brilliantly.

Calm, expressionless, referring to his notes, Corporal Richards methodically recounts almost word for word everything Ken told him about the robbery. Flushed, sweating, Ken writhes with humiliation. His big mouth!

Rick Grenkow sits with his head in his hands. He glances at Paul and John, slumped in their seats. They know what's coming. "Al Clark" was also "Johnny Clark", a sympathetic prisoner locked up with them after their arrest in Vancouver. They had blabbed everything.

"Johnny Clark," it turns out, had help. The rubby with the four-day growth of beard who'd shared their cage appears on the stand resplendent in scarlet with three stripes on his sleeve, Sergeant R.W. Morley. Berry and the Grenkows had talked so much, in such interesting detail, for so long, that Richards and Morley had to spell each other off. Every two or three hours one would be removed from the lockup on the pretext of interrogation. He'd run upstairs to the small room where Richards kept his tape recorder, recount into the microphone all the conversation he could remember, and return to the cage. Berry and the Grenkows told a very exciting story; Richards and Morley had very good memories. It was, Richards admits, very tiring work.

Ken, John Berry and Rick Grenkow are committed to stand trial on charges of conspiracy and theft; Paul Grenkow is committed for trial on a charge of theft and Harry Backlin is charged with unlawful possession of eleven gold bricks.

Ken is denied bail. He is taken to Headingley jail to await trial at the fall assizes.

He won't be there long. In less than four months Ken will embark on his most violent, flamboyant and thrilling escapade.

The
Great
Escape

KEN IS FEELING LOW. He's sick of jail. It's
hot and stuffy in Headingley. The remand cage, where prisoners awaiting trial are kept, is crowded with nineteen,
twenty guys. Some of them stink. Ken's depressed by the
aimless chatter, dirty jokes, foul language. It's September 1,
1966, almost six months since he was put in this pigpen.
Christ, is he going to have to face another ten, fifteen years
of this? He'll go crazy. A year in solitary would be better than
this zoo.

His trial comes up in less than two weeks, September 12.
Ken is pleading not guilty. He's going to fight. All the lawyers
have told him to plead guilty, cooperate, get a lighter sentence.
Less f-ing work for the lawyers, Ken figured, collect a fat fee
after they've put him away for ten years. No way. Not him.
To hell with that lying cop. It was a dirty trick. He was framed.

Ken's lawyer, Mel Myers, resigned from his case. Ken was
broke. He waited more than two months for legal aid to come
up with counsel. In May, John Berry cracked. Pleaded guilty.
Got off with three years. Isn't it funny, Ken thought bitterly,
how the missing gold bar mysteriously turned up at the same
time on the banks of the Assiniboine River not a mile from
where he was sitting in the clink. Berry coughed up the gold,
bought himself off, sold Ken out. Son of a bitch. Ken can

expect at least six years. Add to that the time he still had to serve for the bank robbery and he's looking at ten, twelve years. He'll be almost fifty when he gets out. An old man. Kids grown up. It makes him sick.

Occasionally when someone opens the jail door a breath of soft, sweet air drifts through the fetid cage. Ken can smell the clover and alfalfa and the muddy damp of the river, all the sweet, rich smells of harvest, and he imagines he can see the sun setting red in the west turning the little clouds peach and purple in the turquoise sky. It makes him unbearably homesick for the country, for the threshing gangs and hay-stacks and golden rivers of grain of his childhood on the farm, before everything went wrong. If only he could start over again, clean.

Ken can see the jail door in his mind's eye. It's not more than fifty yards away, just down the hall and around the corner to the left. Ken's been in and out of the jail door dozens of times on his way to and from court. He counts his footsteps every time. One hundred and six. The front door opens directly on to a lawn, nicely kept by the prisoners, with a sidewalk bordered by petunias leading straight to the parking lot. Between the jail and the parking lot there are no fences, no bars, no gates, no walls. Half a mile straight ahead down a gravel road is the Trans-Canada Highway. Prisoners sometimes just walk away from Headingley jail. They usually don't get far. The RCMP detachment is just down the road. Ken thinks he might be the first to make it.

Ken's been planning his escape all summer, plotting it out with the same meticulous care that he devoted to the gold robbery. Heck, there's no work, no recreation in this dump. It keeps his mind busy.

There are three sets of steel bars between Ken and the front door. The first set is the prisoners' cage. The cage contains twenty individual cells where the men are locked up separately for meals and for the night. These cells open into the exercise area where they mill around for the rest of the day. A guard patrols outside the cage. He carries the key which unlocks the door and he comes in if there's a fight or sickness. Once a day each prisoner is allowed to go to a tap down the hall for a basin of hot water to shave. Remand prisoners have an ambiguous status; many have not come to trial and might be innocent. Lawyers and social workers raise hell at the slightest sign of mistreatment or abuse. It makes the guards a little nervous, off-balance, less authoritarian, a little less careful in their precautionary routine. The guards get to know the guys pretty well, patrolling day after day, they trade jokes, gossip, kibitz with the guys on a first name basis, know all their stories. There's no harm in being friendly, keeping the guys cheerful. You can't help being friendly with a guy like Ken Leishman, so good-natured, polite, full of fun, a real interesting guy, a real gentleman.

The second set of steel bars is about twenty yards down the hall, on the left. On the other side is the administration area. At the far end of the administration area the third set of steel bars blocks the front door. Each set of bars is unlocked by a different key on a guard's ring. Ken has tried to memorize the shape of each key.

His sharp eyes have missed nothing. Ken knows that the superintendent leaves at 5 p.m. and the staff is reduced for the night shift. He knows that the guards get lazy after supper, especially when it's hot and sticky and the boss isn't around. He's willing to bet some of them haven't fired a gun in twenty years. There aren't more than three or four guards between the cage and the front door, easy marks for twenty, thirty cons. Ken has his plan all worked out. It all depends on Joe.

Ken took to Joe Dale right away. Joe's a treaty Indian, tall, handsome, right out of the movies. A young guy, quiet, but smart Ken figured, not spaced out like some of the guys. Joe's charged with armed robbery and rape. A farmer Joe'd been working for. Didn't pay him. Joe got pretty mad. Tied the farmer up and banged his wife right in front of him. Not that the wife was anything. It was the guy he was getting at. Took all the cash in the house. That's how he got caught. Bought himself some new duds. What's an Indian doing with fancy clothes eh? Stuck out like a sore thumb.

Ken was impressed by the way Joe could sit there, not moving, not talking, day after day. Ken, he was always pacing, yakking away, mind going like a windmill. He admired Joe's self-control. Strong. Hey, look, it's the Lone Ranger and Tonto! one of the cons yelled one day when Ken and Joe were talking things over in his cell. It kind of tickled Ken's fancy. He decided then they should try a breakout, not just the two of them, no, a whole mob scene, open the place up, free everybody, it would be pandemonium, a hundred guys running in all directions, take the cops days to round 'em all up. Ken and Joe would be a million miles away.

Ken sits in his cell, sweating, massaging his big hands together, eyes anxiously fixed on the bars. Joe Dale's preliminary hearing is today. If charges are dismissed, Joe will be released. Ken will never see him again. If Joe's committed for trial, he'll be back, ready to run. "You ever heard of an Indian gettin' off?" he asked Ken. Ken is counting on Joe. Joe's got a knife.

There he is! Joe Dale is walking towards the cage with his easy, graceful stride, hands loose, face blank. Ken is ready to hug him. As Dale is let back into the cage by the guard Ken sits back in his cell, legs crossed, absorbed in a magazine. In ten minutes he saunters over to Joe.

"When?" he says.

"Now." Joe shrugs. "Seven o'clock."

It's six-thirty. Ken passes the word to the other prisoners. The news crackles through the cage like electricity. Talk gets louder, laughter. Some of the guys start licking their lips, rubbing their hands nervously on their blue prison trousers. Ken glances over at the guard. Young guy. Hard to know what he notices. Seems okay. Ten minutes to go. Ken's feeling good, adrenalin pumping, head spinning. He can almost feel the cool, outside air on his forehead. One minute to seven.

"Hey, Jimmy!" Ken calls, leaning through the bars towards the guard. "I need some hot water, please. Gonna shave my moustache off. Win a bet!"

The guard lets Ken out with his water basin and locks the door behind him. On his way to the tap Ken looks around carefully. Not a soul. All clear. He nods twice as the guard lets him back in. There's a shout from the back of the cage.

"Hey! Help! Come quick! Barry's throwin' a fit!"

Barry is crazy. He's a nice kid, quiet, with a big, homely, raw-boned face and a puzzled look in his eyes. Barry was acquitted of killing his girlfriend on grounds of insanity. Nobody knew what to do with him. He was considered too criminal for the mental hospital, too crazy for the pen. So, while they made up their minds, they stuck Barry in the remand cage at Headingley and doped him to the eyeballs. Only the lieutenant-governor can get him out, Barry says proudly. He scares the rest of the guys. You never know with nut cases. It's not like booze.

The guard runs towards the knot of men gathered in front of Barry's cell. The knot loosens to let the guard through and then tightens around him. Joe Dale's arm clamps like an iron vise around the guard's neck and Joe's knife tickles his armpit. The guard freezes. Ken flicks the gun out of his holster and reaches for his keys. The guard is gagged and trussed with bedsheets and shoved into Barry's cell. Barry is fine. His eyes are shining.

Ken fumbles at the cage door with the keys. It swings open.

"Come on," he whispers urgently. He can feel the men press around him as he runs down the hall. Their sock feet make almost no sound. Ken waves two Indians, Chippeway and Nelson, to take the guards on the upper tier, he and Joe will take the basement. At the bottom of the basement stairs two guards are sitting at the desk reading pocket books. Ken and Joe are on them in a flash, grab their guns, twist their arms behind their backs. They shove the guards into empty cells and slam the doors. They dart back up to the main floor. Chippeway waves at them from the top tier. Everything okay. Guards locked up. Prisoners in control.

George LeClerc, a charming con artist from Montreal, unlocks the remand cage on the top tier. The men huddle back, grouped in a corner like frightened birds. A couple venture tentatively to the open door and stand there, just inside, uncertain what is going on. The men from Ken's cage mill around in the hall, whispering, confused. What to do now? How do they get past the second and third sets of steel bars?

Ken approaches the bars separating the prisoners' hall from the administration area. A guard is sitting at a desk on the other side.

"Hiya," Ken says. "I'd like to see the duty officer, please. I have some information. Confidential. Might be important."

The guard looks up coldly.

"It can wait. See the superintendent in the morning."

Ken argues, polite, insistent, desperate. The men inch closer to the bars, pressed against the wall, just out of the guard's line of vision, poised to run through as soon as he opens the gate for Ken. The guard holds firm. Ken turns to walk away.

Right in front of him, across the hall, the kitchen door swings open. A man in workman's overalls, toolbox under his arm, comes out and walks towards the gate.

"Okay," he calls to the guard. "All done for today."

The guard fumbles with his keys. The prisoners press closer, sliding noiselessly along the wall. The gate clangs open. The men surge through, pinning the workman against the bars. Joe jumps the guard, grabs his keys, shoves him back through the gate and slams it shut.

Leclerc, Nelson and Chippeway are already in the office. They knock the duty officer over the head with his cribbage board.

Joe Dale waves a revolver in his face, pointing at the wall safe. The officer twirls the knob. The door opens and the men grab what comes to hand, a couple of .303's, some .45's, .22's.

"Get the ammo!" cries Ken. "Don't forget the ammo!"

The phone rings. Again. Again. The men stand in frozen silence.

"Answer it," Ken nods at the duty officer. "You'll know what to say."

The officer's eyes rove over the men in the room. There are two murderers in this crowd. He's not going to take any chances. He picks up the receiver gingerly, his eyes on the guns. Ken listens on the extension in the superintendent's office next door.

"Oh? Yeah?" the officer says. "No. No problem. Everything's okay. One of the guards got a little excited. These things happen. Nothing to worry about. Okay. Yeah. Great. No hurry."

"That was the cops all right!" Ken bursts in. "They'll be here in a second!"

The mob swarms down to the basement and breaks down the door of the storeroom where their civvies are kept. Thoughtful of the screws, Ken laughs, to keep the prisoners' clothes neatly on hangers, labelled with each man's name. He grabs his shoes, a sweater and his old fedora.

Ken unlocks the third set of bars. He's first out the door running as fast as his long legs will carry him towards a white Chevy Bel Air, cheap junk, no guts, but you can't expect screws to drive anything decent. He hears panting behind him and the thud of running feet. Funny how everything is so quiet, so green and peaceful, somehow he'd expected noise, men tearing around, yelling, even gunfire. He feels like the first man on earth.

Joe Dale piles in beside Ken as he guns the engine. Barry Duke and George Leclerc jump in the back seat, their legs still hanging out the open doors as Ken floors the accelerator and spins out of the parking lot. He skids down the gravel road in a cloud of dust headed for the highway.

It's seven-fifteen. The jail is very quiet. All eleven guards are locked up. Fifty prisoners mill around helplessly outside their cages, glancing with frightened eyes at the gagged and groaning guards writhing in their cells. A few prisoners peer through the open door. They see the shadows on the fresh-cut grass, the pink petunias by the sidewalk, the parking lot, Ken's plume of dust in the distance. They listen to the crickets tuning up, the hum of traffic on the highway, the sound of sirens getting closer, closer.

Ken has liberated Headingley jail.

Only nine men have followed him to freedom. The rest, held back by bars stronger than steel, wait.

Ken makes a clean getaway, crosses the highway and heads north, sticking to the back roads. Ken is heading for the little air base at Warren. He'll steal a plane and they'll all be safe across the American border in an hour. By nightfall they'll be in the southern states, the next day in Mexico, then South America, or Cuba. Castro will welcome them, refugees from capitalist oppression. Ken has his spiel all worked out.

The sun is still high when they reach Warren. They hide the car in a ditch and conceal themselves in the brush around the airport. It is a lovely clear, calm evening. Small airplanes circle in the sky like swallows swooping down to land. They wait one hour, two. The sky turns a deep sea-green edged with purple. They slip towards a hangar. Ken has his hand on the door when Whoosh! Headlights! A car comes tearing

down the road and screeches into the airport. The white patch
on the door is unmistakable. RCMP. They scramble behind
the hangar and take off through the brush, galloping through
fields, under fences, jumping ditches, stumbling through
summer-fallow, making enough noise, it seems to Ken, for
a herd of elephants. In half a mile they stop to catch their
breath and listen. Crickets. Dogs barking in the distance.
We'll walk, Ken said. Grab the first car we can get and try
the next airfield.

For hours they stumble blindly along the dirt roads, hitting
the ditch every time a car passes. Ken's legs feel thick and
heavy as tree trunks, his clothes are drenched with sweat, his
throat choked with dust. The others pant to keep up with his
long stride, muttering and cursing as they slip on the loose
gravel. Barry falls farther and farther behind. Leave me, he
keeps saying. Don't wait for me. I'll be okay. But Ken won't.
God knows what the kid would do out there in the dark,
dumb, confused. Probably run to the first farm house. Ken
got Barry into this. He'll get him out.

They pass dozens of farm houses but the lights are on and
the dogs yapping. They can't even get close to a well for a
drink. It is a late harvest and the farmers are working round
the clock. Ken can see the combine lights out in the fields.
Lights, cars, people everywhere. They plod on. It is about
thirty miles to St. Andrews air base. If they have to they'll
walk the whole way.

They come across the dark farm house about three o'clock
in the morning. Ken throws a stone at the front door. Silence.
No dog. No car. Sound of running water. A hose is trickling
into a cattle trough. They press the nozzle to their lips and
hold it over their heads letting the cold water run down their
backs.

Joe cuts the telephone line. Ken pounds on the door.

"Hi! Anybody home?" Ken shoves the door open. Yikes!
Ghosts! The house is full of spooky white shapes. Furniture.
Sheets. Nobody home, that's for sure. They find the beds.
Ken keeps watch in an armchair, massaging the knotted mus-
cles of his legs.

He wakes up with a start. Daylight. Wow, wouldn't that
have been something, the cops walking in and him asleep

like a babe in the woods. Ken finds some food in the freezer, berries, hamburger, a loaf of bread. They're so hungry they eat it half-thawed. Tastes great. Barry won't eat. Just lies there in bed, face to the wall. Ken finds $100 in small bills in the family Bible. The rest of them shave, wash and raid the closet. The clothes are okay for George but too small for Joe and Ken. Maybe no one will notice.They are new and clean and decent looking. Joe thinks about dressing up as a woman but Ken laughs so hard he gives the idea up.

They wait for the family to turn up. Ken figures they'll be elderly, no sign of kids, easy to grab. Take off in their car. In the afternoon a small tractor pulls into the yard and a farmer runs water in the trough and cuts the grass. They watch by the windows. What goddamn good is a tractor? The farmer leaves.

They wait. After dark they watch TV, shielding it with a blanket. It is funny seeing their own mug shots on the screen looking like a bunch of zombies. Armed and dangerous! Biggest jailbreak in Canadian history! Flying Bandit takes off again! Ken laughs. It makes them sound like desperados! George puts on a hat to hide the fact that his ears stick out. Joe isn't worried. All Indians look alike, he grins.

They wait. Doze. Just after 1 a.m. Ken is jolted awake. Someone is rattling the door! Lights outside the window. Headlights.

"A car," he whispers to Joe, tugging at his sleeve. "A car! Let's get it."

They shake the others awake. Joe creeps towards the door, gun at the ready, Ken beside him. The rattling stops. The headlights swerve and the car races away.

"Get out of here!" Ken calls. He is out the door like a shot, running across the yard, down the road, then through the ditch, across a ploughed field. He can see headlights coming from the south. Fast. Cops for sure. Take them an hour to stake out the house, maybe longer. He prays they don't have dogs.

The four fugitives trudge once more down the dark country roads.

"Come on, Heather, it's *okay*," Ross Mackenzie whispers urgently in Heather Jackson's ear. His left hand slips down into her bra, his right pushes the strap of her sundress off her shoulder. He can feel her tit getting hard under his fingers. He thrusts his tongue into her mouth. She pulls back, struggles against the pressure. Jeezus, he's got a hard-on that'll split his pants!

"Come on, come on, it's okay."

"Stop it, Ross!" Heather gasps for breath, grabbing at her straps. "Please!"

"It's all right, baby, it's all right."

"Please Ross, I *can't*."

Heather's bare back is stuck to the shiny vinyl seat of Ross's brand new Chevy Malibu. They're parked on a dirt road near Warren, Manitoba, about two miles from Heather's farm. It's a hot, fragrant night, perfect for making out. The hands on the dashboard clock glow green: 1:57 a.m., Saturday, September 3.

"Ross, I've got to get *home*."

"Sure. In a while."

Neither of them notices the four dark figures creeping stealthily along the side of the road. A dozen yards from the car the four shadows stop and huddle together.

"Cops?" asks Barry.

Ken shakes his head, squinting through the dark trying to make out the black shapes in the front seat silhouetted against the pale night sky.

"Don't think so."

Ross's fingers are struggling with the last hook on Heather's bra when the car doors are suddenly flung open. Heather screams and falls half out of the car, Ross on top of her.

"Please," says Heather, pulling at her dress. "Please don't hurt us. Please."

Ken laughs. "Sorry to interrupt."

Ross catches the gleam of Ken's gun in the light from the open car door. Oh, God! Rape. Murder. He's read about things like this. They'll kill him first. He can never take four guys. Run? Leave Heather?

"You can take my wallet," Ross says, holding his hands high in the air. "Not much in it. All I've got." His voice sounds high and squeaky.

George LeClerc lifts Ross's wallet out of his pocket. A five. Three ones. Driver's licence. Good. He pockets it.

"You have nothing to worry about," Ken says softly, "if you do as you're told. Do you understand me? We are going to take you for a short ride. If you and your girlfriend don't make trouble you won't get hurt. When it's all over you will get your car and your wallet back. Is that clear?"

Ross nods dumbly.

"Good," says Ken. "You'd better zip up your pants now."

Shamefaced, trembling with fear, Ross is pushed into the front seat between LeClerc and Ken. Heather is sandwiched in the back between Joe Dale and Barry. Ross is afraid to turn around. God, what are they going to do to her back there? What an asshole he is, big track star, college hero, and he can't even take care of his own girlfriend. He'll never hold his head up again if they ever get out of this alive. . . .

Ken eases the car gently into the centre of the road, picks up speed. He heads north, not too fast, using only the parking lights. The lights of Winnipeg cast a dull yellow glow on the sky to the east. In a few miles Ken will turn east, skirting north of the city and head for the little airport at St. Andrews on the Red River. Fast car. Should make it in an hour. Still time to get away. They'll be in the States before dawn. If only he wasn't so tired. . . .

Ken has been on the run for thirty hours. He is still only twenty miles away from Headingley jail. Ken, Joe Dale, George LeClerc and Barry Duke are the only escaped prisoners still at large. One guy was found wandering around the jail grounds, another was picked up at his mother's house, a third was nabbed in North Dakota. Three Indians were run off the road in a guard's stolen car; they'd spent most of their liberty in the guard's house feasting on beer and cookies.

At 3 a.m. Saturday, September 3, Ken pulls cautiously into St. Andrews. A dozen float planes are moored on the river. A light is burning by the gas pump. He hops into a four-seater Cessna. Keys! Wow! Ken turns the engine over, checks the gauges. Shit. No gas. Risky to gas up under the light. He tries another Cessna. No keys. Could be trouble too, having to land on water. Ken's never flown a float plane before. Not as simple as a farmer's field. He jumps back in the car.

"We're going south."

He should have thought of Steinbach before, rich, Mennonites, pacifists, won't put up a fight, close to the border.

The Malibu speeds southeast now, past Winnipeg. Not a sign of a roadblock.

Joe and Barry are very quiet, staring out the windows. Heather feels better now they've put their guns in their pockets. So far they've kept their hands off her anyway. She steals sideways glances at them. They look okay. Clean. Nice clothes. Not like convicts. Don't convicts have shaved heads? Funny uniforms? God, her mother will be having a fit! The middle of the night and she's not home. Well, it's not her fault.

Ross is more worried about the car than himself. It was a gift from his dad when he won the track scholarship to the University of Illinois. Ross flinches every time a stone flies up against the windshield or knocks against the door. Hell, the thing's going to be a wreck. His dad'll kill him. Who the hell are these guys anyway? The big guy, Ken, seems pretty old for a joy ride.

They're driving through scrub country now, sparsely settled, mostly Ukrainian. The red needle on the gas gauge is brushing the bottom. Ken pulls over on the outskirts of a village.

"Okay, Heather," he says. "It's your turn to help us out."

Ken, Joe, Barry and Ross get out and wait in the brush by the road. Heather slides into the driver's seat, LeClerc beside her, his gun on his knee. Heather drives slowly down the main street. The gas pumps are outside the general store. Heather gets out and bangs timidly on the door.

"Hello? Anyone home?"

"Louder," hisses LeClerc.

"Hello! Hello! I need some gas please!" Heather's voice sounds small and scared in the darkness. What if no one's there?

LeClerc leans on the horn. A light goes on upstairs. In a moment the storekeeper stumbles out, suspenders over his hairy chest, cursing a blue streak. Goddam teenagers in their fancy cars screwin' around half the night! LeClerc holds out Ross's five dollar bill. The storekeeper grunts and rams the nozzle into the tank. You don't pass up a fiver in this neck of the woods even if it is the middle of the night.

The sky is turning grey in the east when the Malibu pulls into Steinbach. They park the car and walk to the airport on the edge of town. One four-seater aircraft is sitting on the tarmac. Locked. In the first hangar Ken finds a spanking new Mooney Mark 21, maroon and beige. No keys. They'll have to cross the wires. George starts to take the dashboard apart. Joe pumps gas into the tanks. Barry says he wants to go to a restaurant and have breakfast. Ken's stomach's in a knot. Daylight now. Seven o'clock. Labour Day weekend. Big shopping day. Let's hope the guy who owns this bird is too busy making money to go for an early ride. George is making enough noise to waken the dead.

Fifteen minutes. Twenty. The dashboard comes free. Ken reaches into the maze of wires. Which ones? One after another he tries them. Nothing. What's wrong? He crosses them in different combinations. Nothing. Jeez! He goes over the electrical system in his head. The circuit breaker! He sets all the circuit breakers. Once more he tries the wires. The engine growls.

"I've got her!" he cries. LeClerc runs up the hangar door and they push the plane out. A couple of cars are parked on the grass. People are standing around other aircraft. No one pays any attention to them. Ken tosses Ross his wallet and car keys.

"Thanks for the ride, kids," he says. "Give us half an hour, will you?"

Ross and Heather watch the four men scramble aboard. Seconds later the plane is taxiing down the runway, gaining speed, lifting into the air. Ken circles low, heading south. He wags his wings at Ross and Heather. They wave. Ross looks at his watch. Seven-fifty. At 8:20 a.m. Ross and Heather knock on the door of the RCMP detachment in Steinbach.

The Mooney Mark 21 crosses the American border at 8 a.m. Then it disappears into thin air.

CHAPTER SIX

Appointment in Gary

KEN FLIES SOUTH over the golden harvest fields. He skims the treetops, flying low to stay off the radar screens. The RCMP will be on his tail by now. They'll alert the FBI, the United States Air Force, maybe NORAD. Ken grins. They can't bring him down with an ICBM. He'll scoot in under their guard, stay off the beaten track, away from the airports the way he did when he was selling pots and pans. The U.S. Air Force is up against the superman of stainless steel.

The Mooney cruises along at 180 miles per hour. A perfect cloudless morning. Farmers wave up at them from their tractors. George LeClerc has no trouble plotting their route from a road map they found on the seat. South Dakota. Minnesota. Ken would be perfectly happy if he weren't so tired. And hungry. Jeez, he hasn't really eaten in two days. Seems like a lifetime. They'll have to stop soon for gas.

He spots a tiny airstrip outside a village. Ken drops the flaps and the plane settles in like a feather. Ken taxis up to a gas pump outside a small shack.

"Cross your fingers, fellas," he says.

An elderly man comes running out.

"Hiya!" says Ken, sticking out his hand. "Name's Page. George Page. Rancher. Up near Edmonton. My boys here. On our way to Texas to check out some cattle. Could use a bit of gas, bite to eat."

"Gee, I'm sorry," the man says. "Pump's not hooked up. Just opened up here. Yer practically my first customer!"

"Shucks," says Ken.

The man wrings his hands.

"Good restaurant in town, though," he says brightly. "Good food, cheap. Hey, lemme buy you fellas breakfast! Treat's on me! Can't let you get away hungry after comin' all this way. My car's right here."

Barry is already galloping towards the car. Ken pauses.

"Golly, that's real good of you, Mr. . . .?"

"Phil. Just call me Phil. Glad t'know ya."

The Chat 'n' Chew Cafe in Tyler, Minnesota is cool and clean. Ken orders for all of them, pancakes, bacon and eggs, toast, coffee. The smell is almost overpowering. Ken tries to eat slowly, not to look too hungry. God, it's the best meal of his life! Heaven! He chatters away between mouthfuls, not wanting Phil to ask questions, talking about his ranch, 10,000 acres in the foothills, pure Hereford, brand Circle K, 2,000 head. Ken dreamed a lot about being a cowboy as a kid, and in jail he often passed the time planning his spread. It all floods back to him now in every detail so real he almost has himself convinced. Phil is impressed, eyes round with admiration. Ken prays he doesn't notice that except for Joe their faces are prison pale.

"Jist a sec," says Phil, pushing back his chair. "Want ya t'meet a frienda mine." He hurries out the door.

Ken's stomach hardens into a knot. He puts down his fork. Joe shoves his plate away. He glances at Ken, eyebrows raised.

Ken takes a deep breath. To run now, in the middle of the meal, would cause trouble, questions. Bluff it out. He shakes his head.

"Sit tight."

They wait, stiff in their chairs, expecting to see the sheriff wheel up his car. No, Phil comes back with a young man in shirt-sleeves, plaid slacks, a camera slung over his shoulder.

"This here's Ralph. He's editor of the Tyler *Journal*. Always lookin' for a story. He'd like to do a little piece about you fellas, sorta talk up the airport a little, yuh know. Mebbe take a picture out by the plane. Wouldn't take a sec. Be much obliged."

Ken looks at Joe. Joe looks at George. George looks at Barry. Barry looks at his empty plate.

"Sure!" Ken booms. "Glad to help you out. Bet our ugly mugs'll break your camera though!"

They drive back out to the airstrip.

" 'Fraid you'll have to count me out," says Ken. "Buddy of mine crashed after having his picture taken. Made me superstitious."

The others stand in a row in front of the plane like the Three Stooges.

"Let's see some action!" Ken shouts. "Look like you're checking her over."

They all bend over the aircraft, peering in the fuel tank, pretending to polish, faces turned away from the camera. Please God, Ken prays, make this a dud.

Click. Click. Ralph asks Ken for his name and address. He'll send along some copies. Ken scribbles "George Page" and an Edmonton address. Can't get out of this comedy any too soon. They shake hands all round.

"Bye!" calls Phil. "Don't rob any banks now!"

"Eh?"

"Dinnacha hear the news? There's these crazy Canucks flyin' around. Broke jail. One a 'em's supposed to be a bank robber. Sure glad it ain't you guys! I'd be a dead duck! Ha, ha!"

The RCMP in Winnipeg is panicky. The Flying Bandit has slipped through their dragnet. A clean getaway. They look like fools. It's after noon, four hours since the Mooney was seen crossing the border. The plane has fuel for three hours at most. It *must* have landed somewhere. But where? Where is Ken Leishman going?

The RCMP matches wits with the Flying Bandit with the same meticulous thoroughness they brought to the investigation of the gold robbery. They know a lot about Ken, his friends, some respectable, some not, his contacts, habits, cast of mind. They know that Ken Leishman never moves in a straight line but always zig-zags, doubles back, takes people unawares, does the unexpected. They know his strengths: his daring, imagination, charm; they also know his weaknesses: his loose tongue, suggestibility, over-confidence, his need for recognition and companionship. Why else would he drag three other guys with him? Why would he take Barry at all? Barry Duke is completely unpredictable when he's not drugged and Barry hasn't had a pill in almost two days. Barry will handicap Ken, slow him down. Ken will likely go to ground. Where? The police sift through Ken's underworld contacts, guys he might have met in Stony, Winnipeg. One name stands out, Paolo, an incorrigible thief and con artist who once cleaned out the till at the Falcon Lake golf course when the cashier turned her back, buried the loot on the tenth hole and played on through cool as a cucumber. Paolo was last heard of in Gary, Indiana.

Flying south from Tyler towards Texas Ken puts down at Okoboji, Iowa. No gas. He flies on to Springfield. Gases up. No questions asked. Coming out of Springfield Ken is feeling cocky. So what if the alert is out? Who's going to recognize them down here? Needles in a haystack. Ken feels conspicuous up in the sky. That's what they're all looking for, the aircraft. Maybe it's time to ditch it. Cuba probably isn't such a good idea after all. Might get shot at. Ken isn't much of a Communist, that's for sure. Some life to risk your neck for. If he tries Mexico, South America, he'll need money, papers. Why not get them here, a new name, new face, maybe a wig? Ken's got a name and address tucked away in the back of his mind, a guy called Paolo in Gary, Indiana. Ken's never met him but he's heard a lot about him. A real pro. Connections. Paolo'll put them on the network. They'll never be heard of again. Gary is right over there, due east.

Russ Shook is discing his stubble field when he hears the buzz of a low-flying plane. It's a familiar sound. Lots of aircraft prefer to use smaller airports at Hobart or Wheeler to avoid the congestion at Chicago's O'Hare. Shook looks up, as he always does, envying guys who can fly for a living instead of being chained to a tractor. Wow! This guy is low! Right over the tree tops. Heck, it looks like he's coming down!

Right on the stubble field! In all his sixty years Russ Shook has seen nothing like this.

The Mooney taxis right up to the tractor.

"Hiya!" Ken calls. "George Page. Edmonton, Alberta. Having a little engine trouble. Mind if I use your phone?"

"No," says Russ. "Not at all."

The Shook house is less than a quarter mile away. Mrs. Shook serves the boys coffee and cake while Ken calls Paolo's number in Gary. Not a working line. Shit! Bad luck again.

"Line seems to be busy," Ken smiles, coming back into the kitchen. Ken talks crops with Russ, whether corn is better for cattle than grass, what kind of yield he gets to an acre, prospects for feedlots, while Mrs. Shook plies them all with sandwiches and pie. They take turns washing and shaving upstairs. Mrs. Shook presses them to stay on until the plane is fixed, plenty of spare room, glad for the company. Ken is tempted. He's tired. His head feels like it's full of feathers. He needs a rest. All the comforts of home.

"Sorry," he says regretfully. "Got an appointment in Gary. Late already. Can't pass this one up. Big deal. Come on, boys. Let's hit the trail."

Russ Shook drives them into Hobart at five o'clock. They can catch a local bus into Gary. Ken says he'll be back for the plane in the morning.

"If I don't turn up, Russ," he laughs, "I hope you learn to fly it."

They get off the bus in downtown Gary at six o'clock. Gary is a tough town, a sailors' town. Ken figures it won't take long to get word around the underworld. Someone will turn up. He'll look for a hooker. Hookers always know the dope. Glad to talk for a couple of bucks. Beats fucking. It's early yet. They'll find a bar, have a few beers. They walk towards the waterfront.

On Washington St. Ken spots a sleazy looking bar, the M & S Tavern. Looks like what they want. Ken and Barry take a table by the door. Joe and George sit near the pool-table. They order two draft each. Then two more. The beer makes Ken woozy. Got to take his time. No rush. After seven o'clock the bar begins to fill up. Noise. Smoke. Ken kids around with Susie, his waitress, a big, fat girl in spike heels, mesh stockings, blond hair showing black at the roots. He slips her a $5 bill.

"I'm looking for a friend," he says. "A guy called Paolo."

"Dunno," she shakes her head. "Don't ring no bells. I'll ask Chris." She nods towards the bar.

Chris, the bartender, hasn't been paying much attention. Business is light. Girls draw the beer. So he's been in the back room watching the evening news on TV. Big story about these Canucks breaking jail in a stolen plane. What a caper! Gave him a good laugh. Show those fuckin' cops. Chris is settling into an "I Love Lucy" rerun when Susie comes over.

Paolo? Sure he knows Paolo. Who wants to know? That big bald guy out there. Says he's a friend. And the little guy with the big ears by the pool table wants to know about papers, you know, passports and stuff. I said you were the guy t'see.

Chris wheels himself out for a look. Chris has been in a wheelchair six years, ever since he got a bullet in the back in a gun fight. He's learned to keep his eyes open and his mouth shut. He glances around the bar. The guy with the big ears is talking to the bald guy. Huh. Seem to be buddies. Why ain't they sittin' together then? Chris looks at Joe. Nigger? Spic? He don't like coloured guys in his place. Chris is sensitive about colour, especially the colour of money, and he notices that the bill lying on the dirty table next to Joe's beer is purple. Susie brings it to the till. A Canadian ten. Chris slips it into his pocket. Sailors carry a lot of Canadian dough. These guys don't look like sailors. What do they want with Paolo? Cops? Rookies out on a test run. Yeah. Chris is going to take his time. Watch and wait.

"Sure," he says to Ken. "I know some people. I'll ask around. Make yourselves comfortable. Next round's on the house."

Russ Shook has also watched the evening news. A regular habit. When the picture of the Mooney Mark 21, call letters CF-RYN, came up on the screen he looked at Mrs. Shook. They both went to the door and looked at the maroon and beige aircraft parked in the shelter of the windbreak at the edge of his stubble field. CF-RYN. Russ Shook walked over and peered inside. A .45 revolver rested on the back seat. Russ Shook called the sheriff. The sheriff put a trace on Ken's call to Gary. He checked out the Hobart bus station. Yes, the clerk remembered them. Four tickets to Gary. One way.

"They were as friendly and polite as you could want," said Russ Shook, dazed. He'd noticed, now that he thought about it, that when Ken went upstairs to shave he had a moustache. When he came back it was gone. Shook had been startled. He'd been too polite to mention it.

By 8 p.m. Chief Conway Mullins of the Gary police has organized a full-scale manhunt for the four Canadian fugitives. He's received a complete description of each one from the FBI. The FBI is combing the underworld for Ken's contact. Gary's reputation for crime attracts crooks like fly paper. It's a small city, only 200,000 people, but it has one of the toughest, best-equipped police forces in North America. Mullins has thirty patrolmen searching the downtown area; another thirty off-duty policemen have volunteered for the search. The Gary civil defence organization is on stand-by alert.

At 10 p.m. Ken is getting worried. They're all getting drunk sitting here. Nothing's turned up. Barry doesn't say much but what he does say doesn't make sense. He doesn't seem to know where he is or why. His eyes are glassy and his hands tremble uncontrollably. Poor kid. Maybe they should call it a night. Ken'll wait until George and Joe finish their beer, then they'll find a hotel somewhere. Maybe he'll take Susie up on her offer of a bed. He's so tired she'll be disappointed. . . .

Through the haze of cigarette smoke Ken sees George go up to the bar and talk to Chris. Ken strains to hear over the blare of the go-go music. Damn! He's given strict orders no one's to talk but himself.

"Wanna buy some gold?" George is saying.

"Gold?" Chris blinks. It's not exactly his line.

"Shut up!" Ken snaps. "You talk too much."

Chris's ears perk up. What's goin' on here? Who are these rubes? Too dumb for cops. The guy with the big ears talks funny. Ain't a wop, that's for sure. Paolo is a wop. What's he doin' with friends like these? How's he goin' to play this? Call Paolo? You might say Paolo is a friend, a pretty expensive friend for all the protection Chris gets. It ain't easy, makin' a decent living in a town like this, hoods, pimps, bootleggers always hustlin' for a slice of the action, cops nosin' in where they're not wanted. The cops'll settle for information, though, a good tip here and there. Chris looks around the bar, thinking hard. Has he got four big fish here? It's worth a try. A tip like this'll keep the heat off for a year. If these jokers are cops, then the joke's on them.

"Lemme make a couplea calls," Chris says to Ken. "I know a guy might help ya out."

He wheels back into his little office behind the bar and picks up the phone.

Ken sits down beside Barry.

"We're in luck," he smiles. "I think we got the fella we want right here."

Chris suddenly wheels up to Ken's table, eyes bright.

"Level with me, will ya?" he whispers. "You guys the jail-birds from Canada?"

Ken nods.

"Listen, they found your plane. The cops are on your tail. Jist heard it on the news. I can put ya up. There's a hotel in back here, the Baltimore. Not much but safe, you know what I mean. Go through the back door and up the stairs. I'll cover for ya."

"Gee, thanks!" says Ken, shaking his hand.

The four run up a flight of broken wooden steps. The Baltimore is a fleabag all right, hooker heaven. Stinks of piss. They scribble fake names in the book, George Page, George LaForte, Mike Hardin and Douglas Brown, all from Sault Ste. Marie. The clerk points down the hall to rooms 236 and 237.

Ken throws his coat on the dirty, sagging bed. What a hole! This is worse than jail. There's something fishy about this place. . . .

Joe slips downstairs and peeks out the door.

"Cops!" cries Joe, running down the hall. "The place is lousy with cops!" Joe darts into 237 and slams the door. Ken can hear the lock click, sound of a window going up.

Barry sits on the edge of Ken's bed quietly smoking.

"Come on!" Ken tugs at his sleeve. "We gotta get out of here!"

Barry doesn't move.

"Naw," he shrugs, shaking his head. "I just re . . . rec . . . reconnoitered. Didn't see no cops."

"Come *on*!" Ken cries. "We can get out the back way."

Barry pulls back, angry.

"I said I seen no cops! You crazy?"

"What the fuck is goin' on here?" A fat man wearing nothing but a jock strap is bellowing down the hall. "There's some asshole on the window ledge scarin' the hell outa my wife! What kinda dump is this place anyway?"

The clerk comes up to Ken waving his arms. "You guys will have to get the hell out!"

"I'll handle it," Ken says. "They've had a bit too much to drink. That's all. It'll be okay. I'll look after it."

Ken knocks on the door of 237.

"It's Ken. Let me in."

The door opens a crack. The muzzle of George's revolver is pointed at Ken's chest. Ken pushes his way in. The room is pitch dark.

"Joe?"

Joe's crouched form appears on the window ledge.

"Get the hell back in here!" Ken whispers.

He hears a strange voice at his back.

"You in there! Get out here. Hands up. You're under arrest!"

Ken steps back into the shadow of the door. His right hand slips into his pocket and his fingers close around his .22. A black shape is silhouetted in the lighted doorway, right arm extended, gun in hand. This guy's in street clothes, Ken thinks. A cop? No. A cop wouldn't make himself a target like that. Ken raises his revolver and takes aim at the stranger's chest. Who is he? Friend of Chris's? Ken hesitates. He feels like he's floating in the darkness, watching himself from outside his skin like he was watching a movie. This isn't happening, he thinks. It's a dream.

George's gun barks in the darkness. Ken feels the bullet pass not six inches from his shoulder. The stranger's gun barks back. Bang, bang, bang. A cry, "Tabernac!" from the dark. George.

Ken throws his gun towards the sound of George's voice and steps quickly into the doorway, hands raised.

"Okay, okay," he says. "I'm clean."

He hears scuffling at the window. George and Joe are getting out. Ken blocks the door with his big frame.

"Hands up!" yells the stranger, sticking his gun in Ken's gut. "Higher!"

Ken raises his hands until they touch the top of the doorframe. The dingy hall is full of cops, big bastards with sawed-off shotguns, tear gas masks slung across their chests. Ken is pushed into room 236. Barry is there, sitting on the bed, handcuffed. Ken's arms are forced behind his back and handcuffs snapped on. They cut into the flesh of his wrists. He and Barry are shoved down the stairs, almost falling, and out into the street.

Jeez! Ken blinks, blinded by the brilliant white glare of the searchlight trained on the M & S Tavern. This looks like Viet Nam! Washington Street is plugged with cruiser cars parked every which way, red lights flashing, sirens moaning, searchlights restlessly sweeping the tavern, the street, the huge murmuring mob gathered outside the ring of cars. Police strut up and down waving guns, yelling through bullhorns, muttering into walkie-talkies. Members of the riot squad, encased like prehistoric monsters in vests and masks, crouch between the cars, rifles at the ready, eyes scanning the windows, the rooftops.

"Hey," Ken says to Barry. "They're putting on a show for us, eh?"

"Got a cigarette?" asks Barry.

They are shoved into a cruiser car right in front of the tavern. The crowd roars, pushing closer for a look. The police link arms and shove them back.

"Got a cigarette?" Barry calls hopefully towards the crowd. Hands go up waving Camels, Marlboroughs, a hail of cigarettes falls around the car like confetti. Kids, quick as monkeys, try to sneak through the police cordon to stick a smoke in Barry's mouth. He leans out the window. A photographer catches him dead on. The cops chase the kids. It's a game now, like a circus. The crowd begins to laugh, eggs the kids on, taunts the cops. Susie waves to Ken from the sidewalk.

"Hey, baby! You shoulda taken me up on my offer! You'd be safe at my place!"

"That's me," Ken grins. "Always in the wrong place at the right time."

"Who'd ya kill?" a man in a straw hat keeps shouting.

"They shot a Mountie!" a woman screams back. "It was on the TV!"

Ken enjoys kidding with the crowd. It takes his mind off the pain in his wrists, the fear in his stomach, the tears at the back of his eyes. He anxiously watches the rooftops. Two firemen in a snorkel—an aerial ladder ending in a metal pod—gaze around high overhead while searchlights probe the sky. Ken can see cops in riot gear scampering across the roof. He crosses his fingers. Maybe Joe and George will make it. Please God don't let them die.

George is bleeding to death behind an air-conditioning duct on the roof of Troxel's jewellery store across the alley from the tavern. He got a bullet in the hand when the cop fired in the hotel. It hurt like hell and made his left arm useless, but he and Joe managed to get to the roof of the hotel and jumped across to the roof of the Gary National Bank next door. They saw a pipe about a foot wide crossing the alley thirty feet above the ground. George shinnied across using his good arm and his knees; Joe ran across like a squirrel. Joe smashed a skylight on top of the jewellery store and let himself down. George slipped and gashed his bad arm on broken glass. Joe tied his belt around George's arm. George crawled to the shelter of the duct while Joe slipped through the skylight.

"They ain't gonna take me alive," he said.

Joe dashed down a stairwell to the main floor. Diamonds winked at him from display cases in the half-light. He headed for the back door. As soon as his hand touched the knob the alarm shrilled.

Ken listens to it in the car. Cops surround the store, crouching behind their cars like an army of toads. They lob tear gas cannisters through the windows. They fire randomly into the store with machine guns. Ack—ack—ack—ack. Glass splinters and crashes to the sidewalk. Six cops rush the store. They come out in five minutes, coughing and gagging. Two of them are whisked away in an ambulance. The whole street reeks of tear gas. Ken coughs and cries, unable, with his shackled hands, to rub his eyes to ease the sting.

Joe has made it back to the roof and across to the J.C. Penney store next door. He fires two shots at the cop chasing him. Misses. Cop misses too. Joe hides under an air duct. He is surrounded and arrested without a struggle. George is already being lowered to the street in the snorkel. He's taken to hospital in an ambulance. Joe is shoved in the car with Ken and Barry. He's covered with blood. It's George's. Joe's okay.

"Got a cigarette?" asks Barry hopefully.

Ken falls asleep as soon as he hits the cold steel of the bunk in the Gary jail. He sleeps for most of the next two days, awakened at intervals to be interrogated, fingerprinted and photographed. He is interviewed by the chief of police, immigration officials, the assistant district commissioner, the commissioner and a reporter for Associated Press. Ken remains aloof, unapologetic.

"We're not a bunch of mad-dog killers," he says. "We're guilty of wanting our freedom. That's all. We weren't looking for trouble." Had he been able to establish his contact they never would have been seen again. He refuses to divulge the name of his contact.

Reporters and photographers descend on the M & S Tavern like a swarm of locusts. Pictures of Ken, Joe, Barry and George are flashed around the world. What a story! Right out of the movies. Even Chris the bartender is interviewed.

"I love life," he says. "I love my country. And I like honest people. I don't want my place to be a place for crooks."

George is stitched back together, bandaged and sedated. On Thursday, September 8, 1966, the four fugitives are driven to the Canadian border at Windsor, Ontario where an RCMP escort waits to take them back to Winnipeg. They ride in separate cars, handcuffed and shackled, each man with a three-man police escort. Ken can't help laughing as the long procession pulls out of the jail yard: four long black limousines, twelve guards, a dozen officials in private cars, a fleet of television trucks and newspaper reporters, an escort of squad cars.

"Who's left to answer the phone?" he asks. "I'm better protected than the President of the United States."

He jokes with his guards all the way to Windsor. In the Windsor jail they're given a cell block all to themselves.

Ken is stunned by all the fuss, the television lights and lines of reporters clamouring for interviews, the microphones stuck in his face, the special guards, bigwigs coming to talk to him, just to *look* at him, people writing down his every word, his face on TV, the National News, crowds of people gawking wherever he goes, pointing, reaching out to touch him, calling his name, cheering. Cheering! Him! That's what he can't get over. It was like this after the gold robbery, listening to people calling in to the radio hot line shows, congratulating him, praising his genius, his nerve, wishing him luck. It swelled his head a little, to tell the truth. Now he can *see* the admiration, *feel* it. These people are on his side. They like him! He *is* a hero!

Saturday, September 10, the four fugitives and their RCMP escort board an Air Canada Viscount for the return flight to Winnipeg. The plane is empty.

"Gee, the red carpet treatment!" Ken winks at his Mountie escort. "We're travelling first class!"

Ken has to eat lunch in handcuffs. He hates it. It makes him spill crumbs on his trousers. But his Mountie is taking no chances. Not in the air.

They touch down at Winnipeg International Airport at 3 p.m. As the plane taxis up to the gate Ken peers out the window at the sea of white faces on the observation deck. Below, airport employees in their white coveralls crowd around the gate staring at the plane. Half of Winnipeg is here, Ken thinks idly to himself. Some big shot must be coming in. A memory floats into the back of his consciousness, a memory so painful he always blocks it out. He was just a little guy, in the country, in a foster home. He can't remember the people's name. The King and Queen were coming to Winnipeg. Can you imagine? The real King and Queen. Everyone was going to Winnipeg to see them. But it cost a quarter. A quarter was a lot of money in 1939. Ken didn't have it. Alone, of all his friends, he didn't get to see the King and Queen. He crept behind the stove and bawled his eyes out.

"Hey, it's me!" he smiles to himself. "I'm the big shot! They've come to see me! Jeez!"

Ken flushes. He straightens his sweater with his manacled hands and wipes the last crumbs from his dark blue trousers. Ken is first off the plane. He stands for a moment framed in the doorway, blinking in the sunlight, grinning, the black fuzz of a new moustache darkening his upper lip. The crowd sways, murmurs. Photographers scurry up to the steps, cameras clicking. Ken looks out over the faces pressed back into the waiting room, searching for one familiar face, a flash of red hair. A line of police keeps the crowd off the tarmac. Dignitaries form a solemn blue cluster to the left, the press beside them, notepads fluttering in the wind, microphones ready. Ken recognizes them all, John Harvard from CJOB, little Hughie Allen from the *Tribune,* all friends. Four RCMP cruiser cars are drawn up in a row to the right, a driver standing by each, and lined up at the foot of the steps, rigidly at attention, stand two immaculate rows of Royal Canadian Mounted Police. My guard of honour, Ken grins.

He takes a deep breath, straightens his shoulders and smiles. Then slowly, deliberately, head high, he walks down the steps. The chain on his leg iron clanks on each one.

The Flying Bandit has come home again.

Ken and Elva Leishman on their wedding day, February 25, 1950.

Ken's mug shot, taken after he stole 12 bars of gold from the Winnipeg airport in 1966. (ARCHIVES, UNIVERSITY OF MANITOBA)

Ken stays out of the picture as George LeClerc, Joe Dale and Barry Duke pose for a journalist with the plane they stole after a spectacular jailbreak.
(ARCHIVES, UNIVERSITY OF MANITOBA)

George Maltby, chief of police in St. James, Manitoba, with the gold bars Ken and his accomplices hijacked.
(ARCHIVES, UNIVERSITY OF MANITOBA)

Ken's three accomplices in the gold theft — John Berry, Richard Grenkow and Paul Grenkow — are taken to court by two police officers.
(ARCHIVES, UNIVERSITY OF MANITOBA)

Police in Gary, Indiana prepare to storm the hotel where the fugitives are holed up. (ARCHIVES, UNIVERSITY OF MANITOBA)

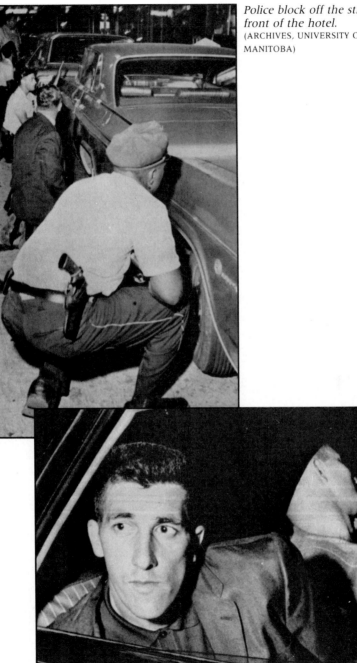

Police block off the street in front of the hotel.
(ARCHIVES, UNIVERSITY OF MANITOBA)

Barry Duke and Ken wait in a squad car while police flush out Joe Dale and George LeClerc from a jewellery store.
(ARCHIVES, UNIVERSITY OF MANITOBA)

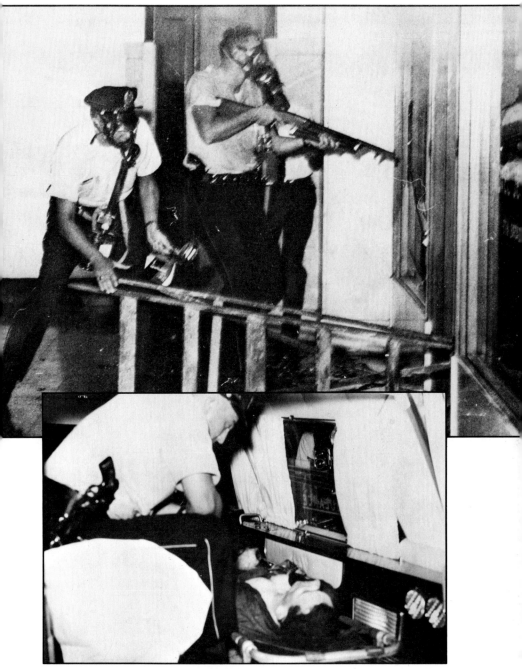

Police wearing gas masks storm the jewellery store. (UPI TELEPHOTO)

Wounded in a shootout, George LeClerc lies in an ambulance after being captured by police. (UPI TELEPHOTO)

Ken Leishman, wearing stolen clothes, is returned to Winnipeg to stand trial for the jailbreak and gold robbery.
(PHOTO BY FRANK CHALMERS)

Looking pleased, Ken gets into an RCMP car for the ride to jail.
(ARCHIVES, UNIVERSITY OF MANITOBA)

The Flying Bandit trades jokes with his captors.
(ARCHIVES, UNIVERSITY OF MANITOBA)

Ken is closely guarded on his
way to trial following a second
escape from jail.
(ARCHIVES, UNIVERSITY OF
MANITOBA)

Ken and Elva with their photo
album in 1978. Ken is president
of the Chamber of Commerce in
Red Lake, the mining town that
produced the gold he hijacked.

The Leishmans with a customer
in The Trading Post, their store
in Red Lake.
(PHOTOS BY FRANK CHALMERS)

The Flying Bandit goes straight — flying mercy missions in Northern Ontario. (PHOTO BY FRANK CHALMERS)

Ken's sons, Wade and Ron, organize a futile search for their father when his plane disappears with two passengers on board in December, 1979. (ARCHIVES, UNIVERSITY OF MANITOBA)

CHAPTER SEVEN

The Impossible Escape

KEN IS GIVEN a whole jail to himself.

The Vaughan Street Detention Home, a dingy old hole behind the law courts building, is the old provincial jail. Its stone walls are thick; its little windows are covered with heavy iron bars. Ken is put in a small, dark cell in the basement popularly known as the death cell. A twenty-four hour guard is mounted outside his door.

"There will be extra guards and special precautions, you can bet your life," growls Superintendent Barry Littlewood of Headingley Jail. The public may think Ken's escapades are a big joke but the Attorney-General of Manitoba, Sterling Lyon, doesn't like looking like the Sheriff of Nottingham. Ken Leishman is not going to get away until the forces of law and order have extracted their pound of flesh.

They throw the book at Ken. With Joe Dale, George LeClerc and Barry Duke he is charged with six separate crimes:

- Breaking out of Headingley Jail, using violence.
- Theft of a $1,000 car, property of the province of Manitoba.
- Breaking into the home of Nestor Ewanek and stealing food and clothing worth $90.
- Unlawfully confining Ross Mackenzie of Balmoral, Manitoba.

- Unlawfully confining Heather Jackson of Stonewall, Manitoba.
- Theft of an aircraft valued at $11,000, property of Abe Loewen, Steinbach, Manitoba.

Ken still has to face trial on the gold theft. It looks like enough to put him away for life.

Week after week Ken waits in his cell while the Crown gathers its evidence. He feels like he's buried alive down there. He eats alone in his cell and he's denied the use of the little exercise yard outside. The cell is dank and musty. The only exercise Ken gets is the weekly ten-minute walk across the parking lot from the jail to the courthouse. He goes as slowly as possible.

Thanksgiving comes and goes. Ken is pale, thin now too, almost gaunt. He looks more like forty-four than thirty-four. He's allowed to read in his cell but the light's so bad it hurts his eyes. So he writes. He writes almost all day and often into the night, covering fifteen, twenty pages of lined foolscap with his neat, tiny script. He's writing his defence, he tells the guard, instructions for his lawyer. It's partly true. Ken's writing his autobiography.

He picked up the idea in the Gary jail. One of the cons said to him "You got John Dillinger's cell, man. That's an honour." Ken had got to thinking about Dillinger and Billy the Kid and Jesse James and all the books that had been written about them, all the movies. People never seemed to get enough. Maybe his story would be interesting too. He'd tell it from the inside, explain how and why he did things, the real dope. Gosh, it might be a best seller, make a million dollars, make a movie, he could play himself! Golly, he'd be a star!

Ken writes feverishly, words spilling out on the paper almost faster than his pen can travel. He's afraid that if the screws get wind of what he's doing they'll forbid him to finish. Can't have a famous con turning into a literary celebrity, making money from his book while he's behind bars. Ha, ha! Writing's a cinch. A piece of cake. Why hadn't he thought of this before. Big money in books. But if he hadn't robbed the banks, stolen the gold, he'd have nothing to write about, would he? And who's got a story like his! Every time his lawyer, Manly Rusen, visits Ken gives him a sheaf of finished pages to take away in his briefcase.

Rusen is impressed. He doesn't know many cons who are literate. Ken is literary. He writes in complex dramatic sentences full of action and imagery. He uses words Rusen has to look up in the dictionary. Sure, the style's a bit stilted, the grammar's pretty rough, but it's a hell of a story. Ken's written more than 200 pages and he hasn't even described the gold robbery. He's pleading not guilty and he doesn't want a confession to fall accidentally into the wrong hands. His trial is set for November 7, 1966.

On October 27, 1966, Harry Backlin is sentenced to seven years in the penitentiary for his part in the gold robbery. Ken's spirits sink. He's sad, slumped when Rusen comes to see him that afternoon.

"Listen, Manly," Ken says, serious. "This place is killing me. I can't breathe. I can't walk. My legs are like water. Seven weeks I've been in this hole. It's inhuman. One more week and they'll have to carry me out of here on a stretcher. That won't look too good, will it? Manly, they've got no right to lock me up in here. I haven't been convicted of a thing. Not a thing!"

Ken's eyes are pleading. He coughs.

"Okay," Rusen says. "I'll see if I can get you out in the exercise yard. How can they turn that down?"

In court the next morning Rusen describes Ken's emaciated form, his cough, his pallor. The conditions under which Ken is being held are "not humanly habitable," he says. The press senses a whiff of scandal. What are they doing to Ken in there? Is he being starved? Beaten? Tortured? They scribble down Rusen's indictment of the Vaughan Street hell hole. Rusen allays fears of escape. Ken is sick, he says, besides "you can't get out of that place with a bazooka."

The judge rejects the exercise yard, but, as compensation, Ken will be allowed to run up and down the corridor outside his cell for half an hour every morning and evening.

The corridor is a narrow tunnel painted bilious yellow. Ken can almost touch both walls with outstretched hands. At one end is the outside wall, at the other is a thick steel mesh door.

The door is locked by an old-fashioned heavy pin-and-bolt device. Ken's watched it a dozen times waiting to be let in and out for his weekly court appearances. The lock is heavy but smooth and well-oiled and slightly worn. Ken's seen bolts like it before, on garages and industrial buildings, rusted often, easily jammed. He's even taken them apart. There isn't much Ken doesn't know about machinery.

Sunday, October 30, is cold and wet. Ken huddles under blankets on his bunk burning with fever. He feels terrible. His cough echoes through the dungeon like a death rattle. Paul, the guard, is worried. He's read the story about Ken's health in the newspapers. Sure, maybe Ken's faking, trying to get into hospital, but what if he's really sick? Christ, the guy sounds like he's dying in there. Paul has grown fond of Ken in the seven weeks of their mutual captivity. They've exchanged pictures of their families, Paul has grandchildren now, and Ken has talked a lot about Elva, how she's stuck with him through thick and thin, kept the family together, the kids out of trouble, his mom too, always sticking up for him, helping out when she could. Paul's never met a prisoner like Ken. Mostly they're foul-mouthed punks, spit at you as soon as look at you, kind of kids you're glad to see behind bars, but not Ken. A real nice guy, smart, knows more about almost everything than Paul, airplanes, farming, selling, even the law, talks about being a social worker some day, helping other guys keep out of trouble, kids especially. Ken's real fond of kids, good with them, too, the kind of guy who'd really straighten them around. Paul figures he'll put in a good word for Ken with the John Howard Society maybe, so when Ken gets out. . . .

Ken listens to the sounds in the corridor. Paul's desk is right outside his door. He hears Paul's occasional footsteps, a magazine being flipped. Ken keeps his eyes fixed on the grill in his door watching for Paul's face. The guards hardly ever look in anymore. It's not decent, somehow, spying on a guy like that. Underneath the blankets Ken's hands are busy. He is ripping his heavy cotton sheets into long, narrow strips, covering the tearing noises with spells of coughing. It's a fairly new sheet, cheap but strong.

He listens for the sound of the buzzer. When Paul wants out to pee, or to get magazines and books for Ken, he pushes the buzzer and the upstairs guard comes down to unlock the door. The buzzer is the only communication between the basement and the main floor. Ken knows by the sound of footsteps and the clank of the door when Paul is gone for a few minutes. As soon as he knows he's alone, Ken takes his hands out from underneath the blankets. He has a piece of electrical wire about two feet long. He'd found it the day before when he'd been exercising in the corridor. Workmen had been doing some repairs to the ancient jail and had left odds and ends of debris in a small crawl space between the top of the cell and the ceiling. The guards were too short to notice but right away Ken had spotted a one-foot length of cast iron pipe. Running his hand along the ledge when Paul's back was turned he'd fingered the wire and swiftly slipped it up his sleeve. He left the pipe where it was.

Now Ken strips the insulated covering from the wire until he has a thin copper strand. From a corner of the bedsheet he makes a small pouch and ties it to one end of the wire with a thread unravelled from the sheet. The whole rig fits neatly into his pocket.

Paul brings Ken's dinner at 5 p.m. Boiled squash again. Ech. The whole jail reeks of it.

"Thanks," Ken mumbles from under his blankets. "I'm not hungry."

"Pumpkin pie," says Paul.

"Help yourself."

Ken is dressed when Paul unlocks his cell for the exercise session at 7 p.m. He is pale, unshaven.

"Maybe I should see a doctor," Ken croaks. He doubles over in a spasm of coughing.

"It's Sunday night. . . ." Paul looks dubious. "I'll call Lloyd Hill upstairs."

Paul turns and goes towards the buzzer.

Ken snatches the piece of pipe, stuffs it in his pocket. He is at the steel door in two strides, his copper wire in his hand. With the pouch in front he slides the wire deftly along the top of the bolt into the locked box where a U-pin secures the end of the bolt. Ken hooks the wire over the end of the bolt; the pouch drops over the pin. With a gentle tug Ken pulls the pin up, the bolt slides back and the door swings open. Paul hears the creak and glances over.

"Hey!"

Ken's hand is in his pants pocket. Paul sees a big bulge.

"Paul, you're a good guy and a friend," Ken says softly, fixing Paul with a steady stare. "I've got a gun here. Your friend Lloyd Hill is coming down the stairs in a few seconds. If you keep quiet and do as I say, he'll be okay. Any noise from you and I'll blow him to bits. Do you understand?"

Paul nods.

"I want you to sit at your desk as usual. Say nothing, don't move. Do you understand?"

Paul nods. Lloyd Hill's heavy footsteps are coming down the stairs.

Ken steps out the door and pushes it shut behind him. He crouches in the shadows under the stairs, watching Lloyd Hill's legs come into sight. He jumps Hill from behind on the second last step, slugs him hard with the piece of pipe in his fist. Hill is stunned but not knocked out. Ken ties him quickly with a strip of bedsheet, trussing him like a chicken. Still the fastest man with a knot in Manitoba. He stuffs a piece of sheet hard into Hill's mouth and drags him down the outer hall. There's a door left open. Utility room. Ken pushes Hill's struggling form in among the pails and mops and shuts the door.

Paul is leaning hard on the buzzer.

Ken hears the footsteps of Hill's partner, guard George White, running towards the stairs. Ken is waiting under the stairs as White runs down. He grabs the guard around the neck and slugs him once, twice with the pipe. White slumps to the floor. Ken grabs his keys and sprints up the stairs. All clear. He takes a brown parka from the office and unlocks the door into the exercise yard.

The rush of cold air almost knocks him over. Ken flings a rope of braided sheets up over the rows of barbed wire on top of the twelve-foot fence. It catches, holds. Bracing his feet against the wall, Ken clambers up. He rolls over on his stomach, the parka protecting him from the wire, feet on the outside now, dangling over the asphalt parking lot, ready to let himself down. His hand gropes for the top of the fence to steady himself, ah, there it is, he grabs hard. Aaah! Pain like a hot knife searing his hand. He pulls his hand away, loses his balance, falls clumsily, left leg bent under his body. Numb, bruised, Ken pulls himself up. Gently he rests his weight on his left ankle. Broken? No, it hurts but it moves. He can still walk. Blood is dripping out of a deep gash across the palm of his hand. He hadn't spotted the broken glass embedded in the top of the wall. Filthy bastards.

Ken wraps his bleeding hand in a piece of torn sheet and hobbles across the empty parking lot, keeping to the shadows. He hardly feels his ankle now but he knows it will hurt later. He's leaving a trail of blood. It's getting dark, no one will notice it. Ken bends into the cold wind and heads north. How far can he go?

He feels in the parka pockets with his good hand. Two pennies and a dime. Not even bus fare. If only he could call a cab, he'd be there before the alarm is sounded. Winnie will take him in. She's a good friend of his mom's. No one will guess. She'll hide him, patch him up, get him out in the country for a while, on a farm, he'll make some money, sneak across the border. He'll make it worth her while. How far is Winnie's? Three miles? Four? Ken pulls the parka hood over his head and close around his face. Have to hoof it.

He walks swiftly north past the Bay, across Portage Avenue, limping, looking for people, a crowd to absorb him. Hardly a soul on the streets. Sunday night, cold, Winnipeg is deader than a doornail. The cold wind helps clear Ken's cough. His fever gives him furious energy. A police cruiser whizzes right past him as he crosses Notre Dame. Not much time now. He heads for the back lanes.

At 7:30 p.m. an emergency bulletin is broadcast on every Winnipeg radio and television station. Ken Leishman, the Flying Bandit, has escaped custody. He is believed to be armed. A city-wide manhunt is organized. Across the city people drop what they're doing, amazed. Can it be true? Has Ken done it again? It's impossible! Then they laugh, hoot with glee. Hurrah for Ken! Let's hope he makes it! Thousands of silent prayers follow the lonely, limping figure as Ken makes his furtive way across the dark city. People begin to see brown parkas lurking in the shadows under the trees, tall men running down the street, they hear noises in the yard. They peer anxiously out the windows.

Police cruisers whizz from place to place, checking out false tips, running down leads, following suspicious looking characters.

"We've got him! We've got him!" A shout crackles over the police radio just before 8 p.m. "There he goes! A white T-shirt!" All cars in the Broadway area are ordered to the parking lot of the Grain Exchange Curling Club behind the Fort Garry Hotel. A man in a white T-shirt is surrounded, slammed against a car, hands pinned behind his back, expert fingers raiding his pockets.

"Hey!" he cries. "What the hell?"

A policeman shines a flashlight in the man's face. Blond. Freckles. Unuh.

"What are you doing here?" barks the officer.

"Curling!" blurts the man in the white T-shirt. "I left my broom in my car."

At 9:42 p.m. police apprehend a man wearing a brown parka at the corner of Ellice Avenue and Furby Street. It's not Ken. A few minutes later police rush to Sargent and McGee where three suspicious men have been spotted. Not Ken. Reports are flooding in from across the city, men loitering, men running, men in parkas, men in prison clothes, men with moustaches.

Ken is in the north end now. It's pitch dark. His hand is killing him. His legs are aching. Elva's face floats in front of him. God, how he'd love to be home. Sit down in a comfortable chair, rest, have a decent meal, just an hour or two with Elva and the kids. Jeez, he hadn't seen the kids in how long, six months? eight months? Just an hour at home. That's all he'd ask.

He stops behind a house on Machray Avenue. Dark. Ken watches. Five minutes, ten. He knocks carefully. No answer. A dog barks inside. He waits, huddled on the rickety back porch nursing his hand. Damn! Trust Winnie to be out. Just his luck. He tries the door. The dog barks again. Can't stay here all night. What does he do now?

Ken keeps walking north, just west of Main Street. St. Andrews is just fifteen miles ahead. He might be able to grab a plane. He's short of breath, his legs are numb. He holds his bandaged hand gingerly in his pocket. He comes out on Main

Street at the Kildonan Shopping Centre on Jefferson Avenue. He peers into a store. Ten-thirty. There's a telephone booth ahead, right on the street, lots of light. Ken looks around. The place is deserted. He'll risk it. Heck, he's only a guy in a parka.

Ken stands in the phone booth fingering the dime in his pocket. He'd like to call Elva. Hear her voice, talk to the kids. The cops are probably there. Tap on the line. He hesitates, rubbing the dime. A car pulls up beside the phone booth. Not cops. Okay. Ken huddles into his parka, pulling the hood around his face. The car stops. Waits. Two guys. They want to use the phone. One of them rolls down the window and stares out at Ken. Ken picks up the receiver, leafs through the phone booth, head down. The car speeds off. Ken shoves the dime into the phone.

"Hiya, Manly?" he says. "It's Ken."

"Christ!" says Manly Rusen. "Where the hell are you?"

"Phone booth. Lookit Manly, I'm finished. Hurt my hand. Can't go any farther. Can you come and get me?"

"Sure, sure! Right away. Where *are* you?"

Muffled coughing on the other end of the phone, breathing, silence. Rusen presses the receiver against his ear.

"Ken? Ken? You okay?"

"Yeah, Manly. Sure." Ken's voice is thick with tears. "Listen, Manly?"

"Yeah?"

"Can you get me out of here? Away somewhere? I'll make it worth your while."

"Come on, Ken. *Come on!* What do you think? I'm a lawyer. Give yourself up. It'll go easier with you. You'll be okay. Look, I'll come pick you up right away. Just hang tight. . . ."

Click. Buzz. Shit! Ken's hung up. Rusen still doesn't know where he is. Oi vey. Who needs a client like this?

Ken is staring through the glass of the phone booth door at Constable Ed Finney's revolver. It's pointed at his gut. Ken raises his hands.

"I'm not a violent man," he says.

"I got him!" Finney crows into the police radio. Ken slumps in the back of the cruiser car. His hands are cuffed. The pain is excruciating.

Finney guns the cruiser car south on Main Street, lights flashing, siren wailing full blast. Wooah! Wooah! Wooah! More cruisers swing in from side streets forming up behind Finney in a screaming cavalcade. Traffic stops at intersections and cars scoot over to the curb to let the procession pass.

It's a proud moment for Const. Finney of the suburban West Kildonan police. Singlehandedly he has nabbed the famous Flying Bandit, the man who's defied the RCMP, the FBI, Interpol, the U.S. Air Force and NORAD. Finney had been tipped off by the two men who wanted to use the phone booth. They'd been listening to the 10:30 p.m. news on the car radio. The man in the booth bore a remarkable resemblance to the description of the fugitive Ken Leishman. They'd sped around the corner and banged on the first door they came to. A woman answered. She didn't want to let them in. It was late. She knew about rapists, robbers, asking to use the phone, besides the Flying Bandit was loose with a gun. That's right! cried the men. He's right around the corner in a phone booth. Leishman! Call 999! Hurry!

The woman reluctantly let them in.

"Why don't you leave him alone?" she said.

Ken is beaten. He's exhausted, depressed, old. He faces, for the first time in his life, the miserable fact of his own failure.

"I'm a bum, Manly," he sighs, his eyes welling with tears. "I deserve to be locked up. I deserve to hang. I'm not fit to live. There's something wrong with me."

He is going to make a clean breast of it. Get it over with.

Tuesday morning, November 1, 1966, Ken, looking smart and sassy in his black suit, white shirt and dark tie, appears in provincial court. He pleads guilty to all six charges arising out of the Headingley escape plus escaping from the Vaughan Street Detention Home. He is sentenced to five years on the Headingley charges, two more years for Vaughan Street. Seven years. Could be worse.

After lunch Ken and Manly go upstairs to County Court where Ken pleads guilty to theft and conspiracy on the gold robbery charges. Ken stands straight and calm in the dock, manacled hands clasped in front of him, his eyes on Elva's red hair behind Rusen's shoulder. The courtroom hums. This is the big one, the one Winnipeg's been waiting for. People have been betting for months on Ken's sentence, anything between ten years and life.

The Crown prosecutor asks for the maximum sentence, ten years, to be added to the seven years Ken has already received plus the four years remaining in his bank robbery sentence. Twenty-one years. Jeez. Ken's hands tremble. He looks at Judge C.I. Keith.

Judge Keith reflects. His face is pale, cold, impassive. Keith is considered a hanging judge.

"I do not feel that this is a case for a ten-year term," he says at last. "I feel eight years will be a sufficient sentence." Keith pauses and looks at Ken, then at the Crown prosecutor. "I am not prepared to make it consecutive."

A gasp rises from the crowded courtroom. Only eight years! For everything! The prosecutor, Gil Goodman, jumps to his feet, flushed.

"Your Honour!" he cries. "Your Honour!"

Keith bangs twice with his gavel, rises and pulls his black gown around him with a flourish.

"Order! Order!"

The crowd shuffles to its feet. Keith stalks out in a swirl of black silk. Ken sucks in his cheeks to keep from grinning. Heck, with parole, good behaviour, he'll be out of the pen in nothing flat. A guard pokes him in the back.

"You got better than you deserve. Let's go."

Ken tries to catch Elva's eye as he's taken away, give her a wink, but she's sitting with her head in her hands, sobbing. The Crown prosecutors are buzzing like angry wasps. Eight years concurrent means that Ken will serve exactly one year for the gold theft. It's outrageous!

"We'll appeal," Goodman mutters. "He can't let the bastard off like that! It's an insult!"

Elva sees the scowling faces, hears the angry words through a haze of grief. Eight years! And they think he got *off!* She rises suddenly from her seat and walks deliberately towards Goodman.

"Go to hell!" she cries, raising her arm. *"Go to hell!"*

Goodman sees the slap coming and ducks. Two policemen grab Elva's arms and hustle her out of the empty courtroom.

On January 17, 1967, in Stonewall, Magistrate Wallace Darichuk orders Ken to serve the remainder of his twelve-year sentence for bank robbery.

The Crown quietly drops its appeal against Ken's sentence. It would only mean more publicity, more notoriety, more fame. Ken is a star. He is better known than Winnipeg's famous mayor, Steve Juba, more popular than the prime minister, Lester Pearson. The more the forces of law and order try to punish Ken Leishman, the more celebrity he achieves. His every word, his every act, good or bad, is news. Ken has moved beyond morality. He is a folk hero.

Who has raised the finger to the establishment with as much flair as Ken Leishman? Canada is flying high in the rebellious Sixties, high on optimism, high on money, Expo, youth, high on dope. Ken is the perfect symbol of breaking out. Up morality. Up the pigs. Let's do our own thing. Peace. Love. Freedom. Ken stands for all these things, especially freedom.

Back in the pen Ken rides the wave of liberal reform like a surfer. Criminology is a chic new science; Ken becomes an expert on criminology. He picks up the new buzz words: treatment, rehabilitation, education. Prisons are wicked; open the gates. Treat animals like men. Educate. Entertain. Integrate. Liberate.

With his instinctive grasp of events, Ken understands, as few convicts have, that prisons are social institutions and therefore vulnerable to public guilt and political pressure. The walls are paper: rules, regulations, laws. Ken studies those rules and regulations and laws with the same single-minded thoroughness he brought to his escapes and his crimes. His attack will be two-pronged. He will attempt to change the rules, and he will look for the loophole which will allow his six-foot, 200-pound frame to slip through the bars. He won't pick the lock; he'll persuade the warden to open the gate.

Ken's first attempt is a failure. When he is transferred from Stony Mountain to Prince Albert maximum security prison in September, 1967, Ken writes a bitter letter to his mother complaining about "sneaky tactics." His high school textbooks have been lost, his personal belongings mislaid, he is hundreds of miles from home and family. His mother, an active, articulate woman in her own right, is on a first-name basis with half the press and radio reporters in Winnipeg. On October 6, 1967, Ken's letter is quoted in the Winnipeg papers under the headline "Leishman Raps Sneak Play."

Letters to the editor is not part of the prison program. Ken is punished. He is accused of attempting to escape and given ten days in the hole. His rare visits with Elva are conducted through a wire mesh screen. His pleas for transfer back to Stony and parole fall on deaf ears. He is told to shut up or else. He shuts up. Ken has another plan.

Both Harry Backlin and Rick Grenkow have been granted paroles to attend university. Why not Ken? He studies day and night to complete his high school education. In 1968 he gets his grade twelve matriculation with high grades. He enrols in a correspondence course in economics from Queen's University. His behaviour is exemplary. He applies to Red River Community College in Winnipeg to enrol in a course in mechanical technology. He is accepted. He applies for a student loan to cover his tuition. He is granted $375. He writes to Justice Minister John Turner requesting a transfer and parole to attend college. He writes to NDP Winnipeg MP Stanley Knowles. He writes to the warden of Stony Mountain asking for his support. He writes the parole board. He badgers his wife and mother, friends, relatives, clergymen, social workers to write letters to the board advocating his parole. He alerts the press to his plans.

Many of Ken's friends are afraid his pressure will antagonize the parole board but Ken pushes ahead. He knows he has the board backed into a corner. Who is going to deny him a chance to better himself? Be a father to his growing boys? A responsible taxpayer? The board dithers and debates for two years. The last straw comes in April, 1969: Elva files for divorce. Ken is transferred back to Stony Mountain in three weeks. The divorce petition is dropped. In the fall of 1970 Ken is granted day parole privileges to attend Red River Community College. Day parole gives him a chance to see his family, find a publisher for his autobiography and chat up the press. Ken is half-free; he's served half his eight years.

Ken's done well, too well. He gets cocky again. Near Christmas, 1971, Ken asks for permission to visit his aged grandfather in Treherne. Granted. Ken packs Elva and the kids in the car. They don't go to Treherne. They go to Steinbach to see a friend who's bought a small aircraft. Ken takes the kids up for a spin.

When the solid citizens of Steinbach discover that the Flying Bandit has been flying again, from the same airport, with his wife and kids, Ken's parole is revoked. He is forced to drop out of college six days before his exams. The story makes headlines. Ken is allowed to write his exams, in the pen, in April, 1972. He passes. He drops out of sight until March 14, 1974 when his familiar face once more appears on the front page of the Winnipeg *Tribune* under the headline:

Manpower Project
CONS GET $93,000 GRANT

Ken has received a grant from Canada Manpower to start an auto body repair shop in Winnipeg employing prisoners on parole. The men have been trained in prison and the project has the support of Stony warden Raymond Desrochers. Most of the money would pay prisoners' salaries. One of those salaries would be that of the office manager, Ken Leishman.

Winnipeg is in an uproar. Giving anyone $93,000 of tax-payers' money is bad enough, but giving it to liars and thieves, and to the most artful thief of them all, Ken Leishman, is too much. Even Ken's most ardent fans are outraged. Ken's application for parole is denied. The project collapses.

Winnipeg is stunned when Ken Leishman walks out of jail six weeks later, a free man.

He calls a press conference, May 4, 1974. "I was detained illegally for seventy-two days," he charges. "There are a lot of men throughout Canada, men with families, sitting in prison, who are undoubtedly in the same position I was in." He is not angry, he says, just bitter about the incompetence of the parole board.

Ken found his loophole. There had been confusion over the exact length of his several sentences. Press reports had been erroneous and parole regulations had become so byzantine that few prisoners could sort them out. Everyone, including Ken, assumed that he would serve the remainder of his sen-

THE IMPOSSIBLE ESCAPE   133

tence for the Toronto bank robberies consecutive to his eight years for the gold robbery and two escapes. It all seemed to work out to about eleven years.

Ken was so angry at being denied parole in March over the $93,000 fiasco he made a thorough study of parole regulations as they affected his case. It was incredibly complicated—an automatic statutory remission of twenty-five per cent in his eight-year sentence, earned remission of three days a month for time served, bonuses, time served while on parole for his original sentence—but when Ken had patiently puzzled it out he came to a startling conclusion: he was a free man! He'd already served all his time, and more!

Ken appealed to the parole board to review his sentence. His time was up, he said. No, said the parole board, three years to go.

Ken appealed to the Department of Justice in Ottawa. The lawyers reviewed his case. They agreed with Ken.

Ken left Stony Mountain for the last time on May 3, 1974, free.

"It is just one of those things sent to haunt us," sighed a parole board official.

The Last Flight

ON FRIDAY, DECEMBER 14, 1979, at the little airport in Red Lake, Ontario, Ken is sitting in the cockpit of a twin Piper Aztec warming up the engine. It's a beautiful little aircraft. Ken would give his right arm to own it. Not much chance now. He's almost too old to fly, a grandfather, would you believe it, six times over! Even if he was younger, even if he had the dough, he'd never get clearance to run an airline. That had been made pretty clear already. Ken had come to Red Lake in 1975 to manage Tomahawk Airlines with an option to buy into the business; the partnership had fallen through. Ken suspected his record. Again. For five and a half years he's been as pure as the driven snow, but to the authorities, to everyone, he'll always be the Flying Bandit. Funny, it was exactly twenty-two years ago today he decided to rob his first bank. Ha, ha! Ken grins, rubbing his hands together in his gloves to warm them up. What was that manager's name? Nice guy. If only he'd taken more money, everything would have been. . . . Ken shrugs, pulls his tocque down over his ears. Damn heater doesn't seem to be working. Can't be helped. This is an emergency. Ken eases the Piper gently towards the snow-packed runway.

The Red Lake runway is little more than a slash in the bush. The biggest aircraft coming in is TransAir's Viscount, known locally as the yellow jellybean, still flying the daily turnaround flight between Red Lake and Winnipeg, still carrying gold bullion twice a month. There's always a cop on duty now. Ken's seen the gold bars a few times in the years he's been living in Red Lake, stacked there on the rack in their wooden boxes with the red seals. He jokes about it a lot with the cops, enjoying their frozen grins. Stupid Harry! Keeping the gold bar in his office! And him a lawyer. If only. . . .

Ken waits for the signal, engines purring, ready to take off for the Indian reserve at Sandy Lake, Ontario. A woman has broken her hip on the trapline. She's to be flown to hospital at Thunder Bay 800 kilometres southeast. Ken's been to Sandy Lake several times. He's a relief pilot for Sabourin Airways of Red Lake, flying when regular pilots are sick or on vacation. He loves the work.

It had been Elva's idea that he become a bush pilot. You like flying, she'd said, why don't you go into flying? It made sense. He loved the north. Bush pilots were a strange bunch of loners, mavericks, misfits. Nobody asked too many questions. That suited him. It would give him independence, a challenge, keep him out of trouble. Besides he needed the money. Fast. Elva and the kids had been cut off welfare the day Ken got out of prison. He had to raise hell to get enough for a week's groceries. Then they'd stuck a lien on his house to collect $3,000 in back welfare payments. Bastards!

Ken borrowed the money to train for his commercial pilot's licence. Then his grandfather died and left him $2,000. Wow! The old man had done something for him at last. Ken finished his course and got a job flying out of Sioux Lookout, Ontario. He was so happy he took all the bum jobs, mercy flights in the middle of the night to airstrips lighted only by the police car's revolving red light, instrument flights in blizzards, all the chancy, dangerous trips the other pilots thought he was crazy to make. Patsies, Ken called them. Ken thrived on the danger, the long hours, fatigue, hardships, unpredictability. Soon he was renowned as one of the toughest, most fearless and dependable pilots in northern Ontario.

Ken was proud of his skill but he was still ambitious. He still dreamed of owning his own lodge some day, once he could save the money. His first lodge, the one that got him into so much trouble, had been taken over by his creditors after he'd gone to jail. They'd let it go for taxes and it was picked up in 1966 by a bunch of Winnipeg newspapermen, of all people, who couldn't make a go of it either. Ken had been pretty bitter about it. What could he do? The place was probably a wreck now. He tried not to think about it. Look to the future. He could start again.

He thought the job with Tomahawk was his big break; in a year or two he'd take it over, build the business, make it pay.

Red Lake was agog when Ken moved into town. Here was the Flying Bandit returning to the very source of his crime, a tiny little backwoods settlement of three thousand people. What was he up to? Was he going to take a whole gold mine this time? What was Ken going to do with Red Lake? And Red Lake with him?

Red Lake took Ken to its heart. He charmed everyone with his frankness, hospitality and good humour. He talked openly about his crimes, laughing at himself, at Harry, at the cops, like it was all a big joke, even prison. He'd come to Red Lake, he said, to start fresh, forget the past. Prison had worked: he was a reformed man. He was a changed man, older, heavier, more relaxed. Weekly sessions with the prison psychologist had made Ken think. Was he trying to punish Elva? Himself? Did he really *like* it in prison? Was it a family? A refuge? Ken had laughed at first—this shrink was nuts!—but the questions had worried away at the back of his mind, casting doubt. Maybe it wasn't bad luck. Maybe *he* had made a mistake. . . . Elva had found comfort in the Mormon church and Ken, although never a religious man, had found a sense of peace, forgiveness, that boosted his spirits and helped channel his restless energy, his frustrations and dreams into more socially acceptable directions.

"I don't hurt any more," he told his mom.

It had been a long time since anyone with Ken's enthusiasm, energy and imagination had blown into Red Lake. Ken was a fountain of ideas. Tourism. Business. Hunting and fishing. Skiing. Red Lake would be a boom town, St. Moritz of Canada. And contacts. Ken had contacts. Cabinet ministers, members of Parliament, radio and television celebrities, business tycoons. Ken dropped names like flies, names of people he'd been in touch with over the years, by mail, from Stony Mountain. Friends. Ken himself was a celebrity. Hollywood actor Darren McGavin was going to make a movie of Ken's life story, Ken might play the role himself, make millions, put Red Lake on the map.

Dreams are the adrenalin of small northern communities where the winters are long, the days short, the jobs dull and the contact with the outside world tenuous. Ken was a dream-weaver, spinning golden visions of limitless prosperity and happiness, visions that gave people hope and excitement even when they suspected, deep down, that they would never come to pass. Ken was a booster too, always looking on the bright side, ready to lend a hand, solve a problem, organize a committee. He made it clear he was in Red Lake to stay, even when he lost his pilot's licence.

Ken blacked out one day in the cockpit of his aircraft just before take-off. He came to okay, in hospital, no pain. People thought it might be his heart. It scared him. Ken had wondered a lot if he wasn't crazy, like poor Barry. Barry'd killed himself in jail in 1968. After Ken was caught in Gary he'd asked for a neurological examination. They'd hooked him up to a bunch of little wires and watched his brainwaves on a machine. He seemed okay. Why then didn't he think like other people? Had one of his accidents knocked a screw loose somewhere? He'd joined the merchant marine on the Great Lakes when he was sixteen and been laid off in six weeks with a ruptured appendix; he'd landed a job as a CNR brakeman after his first stint in Headingley and ended up in hospital after being wiped off a boxcar. It almost seemed as if he was being forced off the straight and narrow.

Ken stuck it out in Red Lake. He and Elva opened the Trading Post, a gift shop and clothing store. It was something for Elva to do now that the five oldest kids had flown the nest, settled, married. Ken was proud of his kids. They'd turned out okay. He had to admire Elva for that, keeping the family together, the kids out of trouble, Elva was strong. It came as a surprise to Ken. He'd always figured he was the strong one. They'd been in Red Lake three months before

Elva twigged that this was the place the gold had come from. "Oh no, Kenny!" she'd said. "Oh no!" But she'd hung in, happy, accepted for herself.

The Trading Post did okay. Ken was still a hotshot salesman. He brought in one of those machines that prints funny slogans on T-shirts, things like "Molson's Ukrainian." It was a big hit. In the summer he'd sometimes take in $800 a day, enough to tide them over the slack times. Ken didn't care that much about money any more. He and Elva lived in a house trailer like a lot of people in Red Lake. It was no palace but it was big enough and homey. He built a houseboat too, a big one, with seats that folded down into beds, and in the summer when the kids were around they'd all take off across the lake for a big picnic. Ken loved to cook, especially steaks slathered with "Dad's sauce," and he started putting on weight. He took it easy, easy for him anyway. A big night for him was a Saturday night dance at the Legion Hall.

Ken got his pilot's licence back in two years. He'd been elected president of the Red Lake Chamber of Commerce in January, 1978. What a hullaballoo that had caused! Knocked Winnipeg on its ear. The *Tribune* sent a reporter up. Ken figured maybe a small notice in the business section. Jeez, you should have seen it! Big spread right across the front page, colour photo of Ken beside an aircraft, headline "Ken Leishman Finds Good Life in Gold Country," two more pages of pictures and story inside. Wow! What an uproar! Why glorify this bum? Bad example for the children. Leishman's a crook. Heck, all Ken had wanted to do was show people he was making something of his life. It wasn't like he was prime minister. Besides it was good publicity for Red Lake. Attract people. Good business. Red Lake, Home of the Famous Flying Bandit. He could put up a sign. . . .

Ken ran for reeve of Red Lake in November, 1978. He lost by seventy-five votes. "People vote very stupidly," he told the press. "If I'd had any kind of machine behind me I probably would have won handily." More than 300 people had voted for Ken. That was something.

Ken taxis down the runway and lifts over the trees, heading for Sandy Lake. It's going to be a long trip. It will be after eight o'clock when he gets to Thunder Bay, no dinner, he'll be tired. A lot of people think he flies mercy flights out of guilt, a need to atone for his past. Ken lets them think that. Actually it's good business. Can't make much money selling clothes in Red Lake, but thousands of Indians live on reserves in the wilderness around. The Bay has their business sewn up. Ken has a plan. He can load a plane with clothes, toys, dishes, jewellery, fly into an Indian community the day the family allowance cheques come out, undersell The Bay and clean up. He'll hit each reserve once, twice a year. Santa Claus. Ken gets along well with Indians. They like his friendly, funny manner. Ken likes them. He is touched by the simplicity and hardship of their lives. It makes his childhood look like a bed of roses. If you do them a kindness they'll be your friends for life. Ken is a kind man.

It's getting dark when Ken lands on the ice of Sandy Lake. The whole community is waiting. Eva Harper is lying on a stretcher. She's been thrown from her snowmobile. Her leg crushed, she lay for more than a day in the bush before she was found. Jackie Meekis, a community nurse, is flying to Thunder Bay with Eva Harper. Ken knows the Indians are superstitious about airplanes. Doctors used to fly in to take away the sick. The doctors came back. The sick did not. Ken promises to get Eva to Thunder Bay as fast as possible.

Ken sights the twinkling lights of Thunder Bay just after 8 p.m. It's a clear, cold night. He can see the lights of the tiny hamlets below and beyond, the vast blackness of Lake Superior. At 8:25 p.m. Ken radios the control tower. He sees the lights of another aircraft ahead. Can he drop to three thousand feet? Go ahead, says the tower. An ambulance is waiting on the tarmac. Ken's Piper is a blip on the radar screen now about fifty kilometres out of Thunder Bay. He's expected down at 8:30 p.m. The ambulance pulls into position near the runway. It waits. And waits. Eight-thirty. Eight-forty. Where's the plane? The blip that was the Piper Aztec has vanished from the radar screen.

Ken Leishman has disappeared into thin air.

A search begins immediately.

At 8:55 p.m. the Canadian Armed Forces search and rescue unit at Trenton, Ontario, is notified that the Piper Aztec is missing. A search operation is scheduled for the next day. A couple of light planes go up from Thunder Bay that night, hoping to spot flares or fire in the dark. Nothing. It seems impossible. He was so close! The weather was good, Ken's voice was calm. There was no hint of trouble. How can he simply disappear like that?

By Monday, December 17, trained armed forces searchers in helicopters and Hercules have joined civilian air patrols combing thousands of square miles of wilderness north of Thunder Bay. It's desolate country, a trackless maze of lakes, muskeg, rock and bush spotted by isolated settlements. The Trans-Canada Highway runs through it like a scar. The Piper Aztec, painted white and black, will be almost invisible. It is not carrying an Emergency Locator Transmitter, a signalling device automatically triggered by a crash. The Piper does have flares, twenty pounds of rations and first aid supplies. The passengers are warmly dressed and familiar with the bush. They'll be able to survive for several days. If they're alive.

Tuesday the search aircraft are grounded by a heavy snowstorm. The blanket of fresh snow covers whatever traces the aircraft may have left when it went down. Already searchers have scoured the area where the radar had pinpointed the plane, hovering low over the ground, scanning the trees and rocks for skid marks, broken branches, a flash of glass, a hole in the ice, a scrap of clothing, anything. Not a trace.

Wednesday, December 19, the search is broadened to a radius of eighty kilometres around Thunder Bay. Elva refuses to lose hope. Three of the Leishman boys, Wade, Robert and Trent are taking part in the search. Family and friends gather round. Darren McGavin asks syndicated psychic Jeanne Dixon to tune in on the lost aircraft. I'll give it a try, Miss Dixon says from Washington, D.C. News of her involvement triggers a rash of calls from local psychics.

By Christmas Day the ground has been covered five and six times. A ground search is out of the question: the ground is too rough, the snow too deep, the weather too cold. "It's hopeless," says search director Major Allen Ditter. The search is called off.

Elva Leishman is distraught. Wade Leishman is furious. Wade is 24, tall and dark and emotional like his dad. The military search was badly organized, he says. Certain key areas were overlooked. The spotters didn't know what to look for. The army is too cowardly to carry out a ground search. Well, the Leishman family will do it themselves. A call goes out for volunteers.

On December 27, urged by Defence Minister Allan McKinnon and Liberal MP John Reid, the military resumes its search for the missing aircraft under a new coordinator, Captain Robert Grant. Once more the area around Thunder Bay is combed. Nothing. The search is abandoned again December 29. It has cost $500,000.

Where is Ken Leishman?

At the back of every mind, and on many lips, is the question: Did Ken Leishman really crash? Or did he just keep on going, south, across the border, his two hostages aboard, the last of the gold bars in his pocket, laughing all the way?

A shaman at Sandy Lake sees a vision of airplane wreckage only a few metres from the shore of Dog Lake north of Thunder Bay. A dozen Indians from Sandy Lake search the area on snow shoes. Nothing. The Indians go into mourning for Eva Harper and Jackie Meekis.

"We can't leave yet," Wade Leishman says in Thunder Bay. "We have to try." Wade is haunted by the horror that his father is still alive, injured, starving, dying a slow, painful death alone in the bush. He and Robert vow to continue the search alone if necessary. "We could handle death," says Robert. "It would be better to deal with than never knowing."

On Friday, January 4, 1980, Wade Leishman, six friends and *Tribune* reporter John Bertrand strike off on a ground search near the southern tip of Dog Lake. They slog through deep snowdrifts, stumble over deadfall, climb granite cliffs, hack through dense brush, inching their way through the unyielding bush tracked by a single Ontario Provincial Police helicopter more concerned with their safety than with the missing aircraft.

Daylight is short, the effort of walking so great that after a few hours the searchers are almost blind with exhaustion. They cover only a few miles a day, pushing themselves on in the hope that the plane will be found just around the next clump of trees, just over the next boulder. Wade's face is gaunt, haggard. He is possessed by the search. "It's something I have to do," he says. "My father had high expectations. High standards. You can't give him anything less in return."

Monday, January 7, another storm dumps three inches of fresh snow over the search area. The OPP helicopter wants to pull out. Bruised, weary, legs knotted with cramps, the tiny band of searchers is ready to admit defeat. Then Wade receives an electrifying phone call.

"I know where the plane is!" says the voice. "I know what happened! I saw it!"

It's Earl Curley, an Ottawa psychic who had once lived across the street from the Leishmans in Winnipeg. Curley has had a vision of the crash. Wade stands transfixed as he listens to Curley's description. The Piper's electrical system went haywire, says Curley. The engine stalled. Ken managed to start it again but it sputtered and died. Ken realized that the safest place to land was Dog Lake. He didn't make it. The plane hit a clump of tall trees near the lake at 100 kilometres an hour. The tail caught on a tree and the aircraft flipped, sheering off its right wing and propelling the fuselage about eighty metres. It nosedived into the forest. All passengers were killed in the crash. Curley says he has been able to pinpoint the exact location of the wreckage on a map.

Wade eagerly scribbles down the coordinates: 48 degrees, 36 minutes north by 89 degrees, 44 minutes west. He checks the map. His spirits soar. Curley's location is only a few kilometres from the spot described by the Sandy Lake shaman. This must be it!

As soon as it's light Wade and his friends are out on Dog Lake looking eagerly for the landmarks Curley described. They search all day, driven by excitement and anticipation. They search all the next day. Not a trace. Wade is certain they've covered the territory Curley described.

"I'm not infallible," Curley admits to John Bertrand. The coordinates he gave were just "a reference point," he says. He might have better luck if he flew over the area. He'll come to Thunder Bay if the Leishman family will pay his air fare from Ottawa. He'll waive his $200 a day fee. He'll only be able to stay one day because he's involved in an international system concerning the United States hostages in Iran. Anyway, Curley says, the wreckage won't be found before January 20, 1980. It will be found by a member of the Leishman family.

Wade is torn by indecision. Tell Curley to fuck off, say some of his friends. He's a human vulture. Sure, maybe he's not charging but he's getting his name in the newspapers. But what if Curley's *right*? How could Wade ever live with himself if he passes up this chance?

"I have a feeling," he says, "that my father is tracking me instead of me tracking him. We just have to look."

Earl Curley arrives in Thunder Bay on Thursday, January 10. He announces that he will locate the aircraft in one hour or quit. He goes up in the OPP helicopter. A low level search over the area reveals nothing. Poor visibility, says Curley. He stays in Thunder Bay over Friday but blowing snow grounds the helicopter. Friday night Earl Curley dreams that Ken Leishman comes into his room, sits on the edge of his bed and tells him that Wade is not looking at all the necessary information. "I interjected," Curley tells John Bertrand, "but Ken told me he only wanted to talk to Wade." Wade, says Curley, had the same dream at the same time. Earl Curley goes home on Saturday.

"Because of losing this individual, everyone in the family will be brought closer together," he says cheerfully. "Although the death is sad the story has a happy ending."

Wade is wrung out. It's a month since the plane vanished. A month of fear, anxiety, chilling cold, endless days and wakeful nights, a month of soaring hope and black despair. His body aches in every muscle, his mind is numb. He feels nothing. He'll rest up, try again later. The search is called off.

The Leishman family clings to the hope that Ken may have miraculously survived, living, perhaps, in some trapper's cabin or a summer cottage with Indians. "If I admitted he is dead," says Elva, "then I would be dead. I feel lost. I feel very scared. We loved each other so strongly. He's alive inside of me."

Elva leaves Red Lake in February to live with Lee Ann in California. She carries with her a poem Ken wrote from prison and reads it every day to keep his memory alive.

To My Wife with Love

Tis a lonely nite my darling
  And I feel so ill at ease
My body yearns with longing
  For your tender hug—your squeeze.

The nights do not bring comfort
  And my days are without mirth
Your husband craves for homelife
  For fireside and hearth.

Your photo is my comfort
  Your smile fulfills my day
And when again I'm at your side
  I'll be there, sweetheart, to stay.

One thousand lonely nights have passed
  Each night brings dark despair
I long so dearly for your touch
  To stroke your silken hair.

I never was a Husband
  Of any great acclaim
I often wonder, sweetheart
  How I sold you on my name.

But the years fulfill their purpose
  And your husband's come of age
Some men mature in battle
  And some within a cage.

Forgiveness is a virtue
  And this I ask of you
I give in turn my life—my love
  Please say that this will do.

Our life now lies before us
  Like a sunset in the west
Tis full of Hope and Promise
  And it's surely heaven blest.

On May 3, 1980, a Canadian Armed Forces search team finds the wreckage of the Piper Aztec in dense bush about forty-five kilometres northwest of Thunder Bay. It had flown right into the trees, shattering into pieces.

"There was no chance for survivors in a crash like that," says military spokesman Captain Philip Anido. "The impact was hard and fast." Death must have been instantaneous.

Fragments of clothing, personal effects and bones are found widely scattered around the crash site.

The wreckage is not where Earl Curley had said it was.

Thunder Bay coroner Dr. E.D. Rathbone rejects a request for an inquest. An investigation into the cause of the crash will be undertaken by Transport Canada, he says. The fragments of bone will be examined by the Ontario Provincial Police laboratory in Toronto to determine the identities of the dead. The bodies, says Dr. Rathbone, appear to have been eaten by wolves or other wild animals.

On May 9, 1980, a memorial service for Ken is held at the Mormon church in Winnipeg. A friend sings Ken's favourite song, "Bridge over Troubled Water." Ken's long obituary appears in both Winnipeg papers. It makes no mention of his crimes. The obituary ends with one of Ken's poems:

The days are long and endless,
And the sun does not take rest.
'Tis a barren hostile country,
And man is put to test
Yet there's compelling remote beauty
In this land so fresh and clean
With its water pure as crystals
And trout that few have seen.
I've drunk of nature's beauty
And I've suffered nature's pest
I've co-existed with God's creatures
And I've met and passed the test.
But this is a land of special beauty
It's a land for special men.
When I leave I'll do so gladly
But I know I'll come again.
I'll bear memories of kind people,

Of sunsets without end,
I'll respect and fear the Northland
And I'll do so as a friend.

Epilogue

THE MYSTERY OF the Flying Bandit's disappearance has never been solved.

Ken's body has never been found.

At an inquest on December 16, 1980, almost exactly a year after the crash, Ken Leishman was declared officially dead. Searchers reported that fragments of Ken's clothing and some personal effects had been found at the crash site; however, a couple of fragments of bone believed by forensic scientists to be male could not be positively identified as Ken's.

The cause of the crash has not been determined. Investigators with Transport Canada speculated that a fuel diaphragm might have ruptured in flight; they also suggested Ken might have made an error in estimating his altitude. "As he was coming down, something may have happened in the aircraft and he may have misread the altimeter," Clyde Johnson told the jury. Even the best pilots make mistakes in judgement, he said. The Piper crashed into the bush at 150 knots, shattering on impact. Only the tail section was left intact.

Bones, clothing, even seatbelts found at the site had been gnawed by animals. Investigators concluded that the bodies, including Ken's, had been devoured during the four months between the crash and the time the wreckage was spotted.

The inquest was called because many people in Winnipeg refused to believe Ken Leishman was dead. He had disappeared before. Besides, the six-pound piece of gold Ken stashed near the Vancouver airport in 1966 has never turned up, has it? At prices running close to $700 an ounce, that piece of gold would be worth more than $50,000. A good grubstake for a new life. Rumours flew that Ken had parachuted out of the plane and taken off for a secret destination, or that he had simply walked away from the crash, never to be seen again.

Investigator Clyde Johnson dismissed rumours of a parachute jump. It would be almost impossible to open the door of a Piper in flight, he said. Had it happened, the path of the plane as it crashed into the trees would have looked much different. Wade Leishman also said that his father had no reason to disappear. "There was nothing to gain by his absence," he told the inquest. "He had no insurance, no motive whatsoever. He had too much to value in life to ever have jumped from that plane and left those two women there. In all the things he did, he never harmed anyone."

The jury recommended that small aircraft be painted in bright colours and carry Emergency Locator Transmitters: the Canadian Armed Forces rescue planes had flown over the crash site nineteen times without spotting the plane.

Is Ken Leishman dead? Or has he pulled his last great caper? Could he have found some astonishing way of disappearing? It seems impossible, incredible, yet Ken has done the impossible before. With Ken Leishman you take nothing for granted.

Ken was growing a beard when he disappeared. He looked completely different. He talked about trying to sneak across the border to visit Lee Ann in California for Christmas. He had a disguise.

Will Ken turn up, in a year or two or ten, in Rio or Buenos Aires or Hong Kong, rich, cocky as ever, with that wide grin and roguish twinkle in his eye that says "Ha, ha! Fooled you again!"

Who knows?

In the memories of those who knew him, loved him, raged at him, chased him, guarded him, helped him, defended him and outwitted him, in the folklore of Canada, The Flying Bandit will live forever.